RAISING THEM RIGHT

Raising Them Right

Focus on the Family
Offers Its Best Advice on Child-Rearing

PUBLISHING
Colorado Springs, Colorado

Published by Focus on the Family Publishing,
Colorado Springs, Colorado 80995
Distributed by Word Books, Dallas, Texas.

Editor: Mike Yorkey
Designer: Multnomah Graphics

Printed in the United States of America

CONTENTS

Foreword

PART FOUR: FOCUS ON DIFFICULT FAMILY PROBLEMS

PART FIVE: FOCUS ON EDUCATION

PART SIX: FOCUS ON FAMILY ACTIVITIES

FOREWORD

One of the best parts of my job as editor of *Focus on the Family* magazine is spending time with reader mail. I can still recall the time this letter crossed my desk several years ago:

I was deeply touched to read the story of how a father and mother helped their children make a commitment to God to remain sexually pure until marriage.

Being a great file maker, I recently started one for my little boy. I use it not only to store medical records and his social security number, but I also add articles that I think will help him (and me) in years to come.

I've removed the article on keeping your teens sexually pure and safely filed it away. No doubt, I will reread it several times before my boy is ready for his own "key talk."

Isn't that a great letter? We know this mom is not the only parent who saves favorite articles from *Focus on the Family* magazine—our mail tells us that. That's why we are publishing *Raising Them Right*, a compilation of our best material on parenting. You'll find 37 articles in eight different categories all together in one place.

In case you're not familiar with the ministry of Focus on the Family, we're here to serve parents and their children. Successful family living has always required time, attention, and effort. And with all the social upheaval of the last three decades, the task hasn't gotten any easier.

Dr. James Dobson, a noted family psychologist and author of 13 best-selling books, founded Focus on the Family in 1977. Since its beginning, the non-profit organization has been committed to supporting families with the information and encouragement they need.

That's why you'll find a lot of practical information and solid encouragement in the pages of this book. We hope *Raising Them Right* is a resource you'll want to pick up again and again.

—Mike Yorkey
Editor of *Focus on the Family* magazine

PART ONE

FOCUS ON RAISING CHILDREN

❦ 1

Dare to Discipline—in the '90s

James C. Dobson, Ph.D.

*T*he first edition of *Dare to Discipline* was written in the early 1970s when I was a professor of pediatrics at the University of Southern California School of Medicine. Our own children, Danae and Ryan, were still preschoolers, which made it risky to offer advice about parenting techniques. That's like a coach bragging in the first quarter about how he expects to win the game.

Nevertheless, I had seen enough academically and professionally to have developed some firm convictions about how children should be raised and what they needed from their parents.

The passage of time has broadened my horizon and, hopefully, sharpened my vision. I've worked with thousands of families, and I've

3

considered the child-rearing views of many authorities and colleagues. My kids have paddled through adolescence and have established homes of their own. Thus, it is a special privilege for me to roll back the clock now and revisit the themes with which I first grappled so many years ago.

One might expect my views of child development and parenting to have evolved significantly within the intervening years. Such is not the case. Admittedly, the social backdrop for the original *Dare to Discipline* has changed dramatically, which is why the book needed to be revised and expanded. The student revolution that raged through the late '60s and early '70s has subsided. Woodstock and the Vietnam War are distant memories, and university campuses are again quieter and less rebellious.

But children haven't changed, nor will they ever. I'm even more convinced now that the principles of good parenting are eternal, having originated with the Creator of families. The inspired concepts in Scripture have been handed down generation after generation and are just as valid for the 21st century as they were for our ancestors.

A Defiant Three-Year-Old

Unfortunately, many of today's parents have never heard those time-honored ideas and have no clue about what they're trying to accomplish at home.

I'll never forget a mother who asked for my help in handling her defiant three-year-old daughter, Sandy. She realized that her tiny little girl had hopelessly beaten her in a contest of wills, and the child had become a tyrant and a dictator. One afternoon, the mother (I'll call her Mrs. Nichols) put the youngster down for a nap, but she knew it was unlikely she would stay in bed. Sandy was not accustomed to doing anything she didn't fancy, and nap time was not on her list of fun things to do in the afternoon.

On this occasion, however, the child was more interested in antagonizing her mom than in merely having her own way. Sandy began to scream. She yelled loudly enough to upset the whole neighborhood, fraying Mrs. Nichols's jangled nerves. Then she tearfully demanded various things, including a glass of water.

At first Mrs. Nichols refused to comply with the orders, but she surrendered when Sandy's screaming again reached a peak of intensity.

As the glass of water was delivered, the mischievous child pushed it aside, refusing to drink because her mother had not brought it soon enough. Mrs. Nichols stood offering the water for a few minutes, then said she would take it back to the kitchen if Sandy did not drink by the time she counted to five.

Sandy set her jaw and waited through the count: "three . . . four . . . five!" As Mrs. Nichols grasped the glass and walked toward the kitchen, the child screamed for the water. Sandy dangled her harassed mom back and forth like a yo-yo until she tired of the sport.

Mrs. Nichols and her little daughter are among the many casualties of an unworkable, illogical philosophy of child management that has long dominated the literature on this subject. This mother had read that a child will eventually respond to reason and forbearance, ruling out the need for firm leadership. She had been told to encourage the child's rebellion because it offered a valuable release of hostility.

Unfortunately, Mrs. Nichols and her advisors were wrong! She and her child were involved in no simple difference of opinion: She was being challenged, mocked, and defied by her daughter. No heart-to-heart talk would resolve this nose-to-nose confrontation, because the real issue was totally unrelated to water or the nap.

The actual meaning behind this conflict and a hundred others was simply this: Sandy was brazenly rejecting the authority of her mother. The way Mrs. Nichols handled these confrontations would determine the nature of their future relationship, especially during the adolescent years.

Where Are the Boundaries?

Much has been written about the dangers of harsh, oppressive, unloving discipline; these warnings are valid and should be heeded.

However, the consequences of oppressive discipline have been cited as justification for the abdication of leadership. That is foolish.

There are times when a strong-willed child will clench his little fists and dare his parents to accept his challenges. He is not motivated by frustration or inner hostility, as is often supposed. He merely wants to know where the boundaries lie and who's available to enforce them.

Mrs. Nichols and all her contemporaries need to know how to set limits and what to do when defiant behavior occurs. This disciplinary activity must take place within the framework of love and affection, which is often difficult for parents who view these roles as contradictory.

Children thrive best in an atmosphere of genuine love, under-girded by reasonable, consistent discipline. In a day of widespread drug usage, immorality, sexually transmitted diseases, vandalism, and violence, we must not depend on hope and luck to fashion the critical attitudes we value in our children.

Permissiveness has not simply failed as an approach to child rearing. It's been a *disaster* for those who have tried it.

When properly applied, loving discipline works! It stimulates tender affection, made possible by *mutual* respect between a parent and a child. It bridges the gap that otherwise separates family members who should love and trust each other. It allows the God of our ancestors to be introduced to our beloved children. It permits teachers to do the kind of job in classrooms for which they are commissioned. It encourages a child to respect other people and live as a responsible, constructive citizen.

The Ability to Lead

As might be expected, there is a price tag on these benefits: They require courage, consistency, conviction, diligence, and enthusiastic effort. In short, one must *dare to discipline* in an environment of unmitigated love.

Many of the writers offering their opinions on this subject in recent years have confused parents, stripping them of the ability to lead in their own homes. They have failed to acknowledge the desire of most youngsters to rule their own lives and prevail in the contest of wills that typically occurs between generations.

A parenting text entitled *Your Child from Two to Five*, published during the permissive 1950s, included this bit of advice paraphrased from the writings of a Dr. Luther Woodward:

> *What do you do when your preschooler calls you a "big stinker" or threatens to flush you down the toilet? Do you scold . . . punish . . . or sensibly take it in stride? Dr. Woodward recommends a positive policy of understanding as the best and fastest way to help a child outgrow this verbal violence. When parents fully realize that all little tots feel angry and destructive at times, they are better able to minimize these outbursts.*
>
> *Once the preschooler gets rid of his hostility, the desire to destroy is gone and instinctive feelings of love and affection have a chance to sprout and grow. Once the child is 6 or 7, parents can rightly let the child know that he is expected to be outgrowing sassing his parents.*

Having offered that sage advice, with which I disagree strongly, Dr. Woodward then told parents to brace themselves for unjust criticism. He wrote, "But this policy [of letting children engage in defiance] takes a broad perspective and a lot of composure, especially when friends and relatives voice disapproval and warn that you are bringing up a brat."

In this case, your friends and relatives will probably be right. Dr. Woodward's recommendation is typical of the advice given to parents in the mid-20th century. It encouraged them to stand passively through the formative years when respect for authority can so easily be taught. I responded to that counsel this way in my book *The Strong-Willed Child*:

> *Dr. Woodward's suggestion is based on the simplistic notion that children will develop sweet and loving attitudes if we adults*

will permit and encourage their temper tantrums during child-hood. According to the optimistic Dr. Woodward, the tot who has been calling his mother a "big stinker" for six or seven years can be expected to embrace her suddenly in love and dignity.

That outcome is most improbable. Dr. Woodward's creative "policy of understanding" (which means stand and do nothing) offers a one-way ticket to adolescent rebellion in many cases.

I believe that if it is desirable for children to be kind, appreciative and pleasant, those qualities should be taught—not hoped for.

If we want to see honesty, truthfulness and unselfishness in our offspring, then these characteristics should be the conscious objectives of our early instructional process. The point is obvious: Heredity does not equip a child with proper attitudes; children learn what they are taught. We cannot expect the coveted behavior to appear magically if we have not done our early homework.

The advice Dr. Woodward and others have offered to parents through the years has led to a type of paralysis in dealing with their kids. In the absence of "permission" to step in and lead, mothers and fathers were left with only their anger and frustration in response to defiant behavior.

The best source of guidance for parents can be found in the wisdom of the Judeo-Christian ethic, which originated with the Creator and was then handed down generation by generation from the time of Christ.

God has given us the assignment of representing Him during the formative years of parenting. That's why it is so critically important for us to acquaint our kids with God's two predominant natures: His unfathomable love and His justice. If we love our children but permit them to treat us disrespectfully and with disdain, we have distorted their understanding of the Father.

On the other hand, if we are rigid disciplinarians who show no love, we have tipped the scales in the other direction. What we teach our children about the Lord is a function, to some degree, of how we model love and discipline in our relationship with them. Scary, huh?

Challenges to Authority

The issue of respect is also useful in guiding parents' interpretations of given behavior. First, they should decide whether an undesirable act represents a direct challenge to their authority . . . to their leadership positions as fathers or mothers. The form of disciplinary action they should take depends on the result of that evaluation.

For example, suppose little Chris is acting silly in the living room and falls into a table, breaking several expensive china cups and other trinkets. Or suppose Wendy loses her bicycle or leaves her mother's coffeepot out in the rain. These are acts of childish irresponsibility and should be handled as such. Perhaps the parent will ignore the event or maybe have the child work to pay for the losses—depending on his age and maturity, of course.

However, these examples do not constitute direct challenges to authority. They do not emanate from willful, haughty disobedience and, therefore, should not result in serious discipline. In my opinion, spankings should be reserved for the moment a child (between the age of 18 months to 10 years old) expresses to parents a defiant "I will not!" or "You shut up!" When youngsters convey this kind of stiff-necked rebellion, you must be willing to respond to the challenge immediately. When nose-to-nose confrontation occurs between you and your child, it is not the time to discuss the virtues of obedience. It is not the occasion to send him to his room to pout. Nor is it appropriate to postpone disciplinary measures until your tired spouse plods home from work.

You have drawn a line in the dirt, and the child has deliberately flopped his little pink toe across it. Who is going to win? Who has the most courage? Who is in charge here? If you do not conclusively answer these questions for your strong-willed children, they will precipitate other battles designed to ask them again and again. It is the ultimate paradox of childhood that youngsters want to be led, but insist that their parents earn the right to lead them.

When mothers and fathers fail to take charge in moments of challenge, they create for themselves and their families a potential lifetime of heartache. That's what happened in the case of the Holloways, who were the parents of a teen named Becky (not their real names). Mr. Holloway came to see me in desperation one afternoon. Becky had never been required to obey or respect her parents, and her early years were a strain on the entire family. Mrs. Holloway thought Becky would eventually become manageable, but that never happened. She held her parents in contempt and was disrespectful and uncooperative. Mr. and Mrs. Holloway did not feel they had the right to make demands on their daughter, so they smiled politely and pretended not to notice her horrid behavior.

Their magnanimous attitude became more difficult to maintain as Becky steamrolled into puberty and adolescence. Mr. and Mrs. Holloway were afraid to antagonize her because she would throw violent tantrums. They were victims of emotional blackmail. Once, they installed a telephone in her room. She accepted it without gratitude and accumulated a staggering bill during the first month of usage.

They thought a party might make her happy, and Mrs. Holloway worked hard to decorate the house and prepare refreshments. On the appointed evening, a mob of dirty, profane teens swarmed into the house, destroying the furnishings. During the evening, Mrs. Holloway said something that angered Becky. The girl struck her mother and left her lying in a pool of blood.

Mr. Holloway found his wife helpless on the floor and located his daughter dancing with friends. As he described for me the details of their recent nightmare, he spoke with tears in his eyes. Parents like the Holloways often fail to understand how love and discipline interact to influence the attitudes of a child. These two aspects of a relationship are not opposites working against each other. One demands the other.

Disciplinary action is not an assault on parental love; it is a function of it. Appropriate punishment is not something parents do *to* a beloved child; it is something done *for* him or her. That simple understanding when Becky was younger could have spared the Holloways an adolescent nightmare.

To repeat, the objective of disciplining a child is to gain and maintain his respect. If the parents fail in this task, life becomes uncomfortable indeed.

❧ ❧ ❧

Spanking: Helpful or Harmful?

Q. Do you think you should spank a child for every act of disobedience or defiance?

A. No. Corporal punishment should be a rather infrequent occurrence. There is an appropriate time for a child to sit on a chair to "think" about his misbehavior, or he might be deprived of a privilege, or sent to his room for a "time out," or made to work when he had planned to play. In other words, you should vary your response to misbehavior, always hoping to stay one step ahead of the child.

Q. Where would you administer a spanking?

A. It should be confined to the buttocks area, where permanent damage is very unlikely. I do not believe in slapping a child on the face or in jerking him around by the arms. A common form of injury I saw in the emergency room at Children's Hospital involved children with shoulder separations. Parents had pulled tiny arms angrily and dislocated the shoulder or elbow. If you spank a child only on the "behind" or on the upper part of the legs, I think you will be doing it right.

Q. Do you think corporal punishment will eventually be outlawed?

A. It is very likely. The tragedy of child abuse has made it difficult for people to understand the difference between viciousness to kids and constructive, positive forms of physical punishment. There are those in the Western world who will not rest until the government interferes with parent-child relationships with all the force of law.

It has already happened in Sweden, and the media seems determined to bring that legislation to the United States. It will be a sad day for families. Child abuse will increase, not decrease, as frustrated parents explode after having no appropriate response to defiant behavior.

Q. There is some controversy over whether a parent should spank with his or her hand or with some other object, such as a belt or paddle. What do you recommend?

A. I recommend a neutral object of some type. To those who disagree on this point, I'd encourage them to do what seems right to them. It is not a critical issue to me. The reason I suggest a switch or paddle is because the hand should be seen as an object of love—to hold, hug, pat, and caress. However, if you're used to suddenly disciplining with the hand, your child may not know when he's about to be swatted and can develop a pattern of flinching when you suddenly scratch your head. This is not a problem if you take the time to get a neutral object.

Q. Is there an age when you begin to spank? And at what age do you stop?

A. There is no excuse for spanking babies or children younger than 15 to 18 months of age. Even shaking an infant can cause brain damage and death at this delicate age! But midway through the second year (18 months), a boy or girl becomes capable of knowing what you're telling them to do or not to do. They can then very gently be held responsible for how they behave.

Suppose a child is reaching for an electric socket or something that will hurt him. You say, "No!" but he just looks at you and continues reaching toward it. You can see the smile of challenge on his face as he thinks, *I'm going to do it anyway!* I'd encourage you to thump his fingers just enough to sting. A small amount of pain goes a long way at that age and begins to introduce children to realities of the world and the importance of listening to what you say.

There is no magical time at the end of childhood when spanking becomes ineffective, because children vary so much emotionally and developmentally. But as a general guideline, I would suggest that *most* corporal punishment be finished prior to the first grade (six years old). It should taper off from there and stop when the child is between the ages of 10 and 12.

Q. I have never spanked my three-year-old because I am afraid it will teach her to hit others and be a violent person. Do you think I am wrong?

A. You have asked a vitally important question that reflects a common misunderstanding about child management. First, let me emphasize that it *is* possible . . . even easy . . . to create a violent and aggressive child who has observed this behavior at home. If he is routinely beaten by hostile, volatile parents, or if he witnesses physical violence between angry adults, or if he feels unloved and unappreciated within his family, the child will not fail to notice how the game is played.

Thus, corporal punishment that is not administered according to very carefully thought-out guidelines is a dangerous thing. Being a parent carries *no* right to slap and intimidate a child because you had a bad day or are in a lousy mood. It is this kind of unjust discipline that causes some well-meaning authorities to reject corporal punishment altogether.

Just because a technique is used wrongly, however, is no reason to reject it altogether. Many children desperately need this resolution to their disobedience.

When he lowers his head, clenches his fists, and makes it clear he is going for broke, justice must speak swiftly and eloquently. Not only does this response not create aggression in a boy or girl, it helps them control their impulses and live in harmony with various forms of benevolent authority throughout life. Why? Because it is in harmony with nature itself. Consider the purpose of minor pain in a child's life.

Suppose two-year-old Peter touches a hot stove. From that experience, he quickly learns that heat must be respected. If he lives to be 100, he will never again reach out and touch the red-hot coils of a stove.

The same lesson is learned when he pulls the doggy's tail and promptly receives a neat row of teeth marks across the back of his hand, or when he climbs out of his high chair when Mom isn't looking and discovers all about gravity.

For three or four years, he accumulates bumps, bruises, scratches, and burns, each one teaching him about life's boundaries. Do these experiences make him a violent person? No! The pain associated with these events teaches him to avoid making the same mistakes again. God created this mechanism as a valuable vehicle for instruction.

Now when a parent administers a reasonable spanking in response to willful disobedience, a similar nonverbal message is being given to the child. He must understand that there are not only dangers in the physical world to be avoided. He should also be wary of dan-

gers in his social world, such as defiance, sassiness, self-
ishness, temper tantrums, behavior that puts his life in
danger, etc. The minor pain that is associated with this
deliberate misbehavior tends to inhibit it, just as discomfort works to shape behavior in the physical world.

Dr. Dobson holds a Ph.D. in child development from the University of Southern
California and five honorary doctorates from Pepperdine University, Franciscan
University in Steubenville, Seattle Pacific University, Asbury Seminary, and Mid-
America Nazarene Seminary. He is the father of two grown children and resides in
Colorado Springs with his wife, Shirley. This chapter is adapted from *The New Dare
to Discipline* Dr. James Dobson, 1970, 1992. Used by permission of Tyndale House
Publishers, Inc. All rights reserved.

2

Two Swords
of Power

Gary Smalley and John Trent, Ph.D.

ohn and his friend, Ty, were talking over coffee after their 20th
high school reunion. "You just can't imagine the feeling," Ty
said. "Flying an F-16 is the closest thing you can get to being
strapped onto a guided missile."

Ty was the flight leader of an Air Force quick-deployment fighter
group. Now a veteran pilot and a still-youthful Air Force major, he
had all the positional power a man could ask for. He was respected by
those ranking above him, saluted by everyone under him, and
counted on by those who flew with him.

He was also losing his family.

All his training as an elite Air Force officer never prepared him for
the quiet warfare on the home front. His eyes reflected pain and helpless frustration. The same power that helped him win the war in the
Gulf had destroyed his family.

He remembered ruefully all the times he openly resented being at home instead of hanging out at the air base. All those broken promises of weekend trips and romantic dinners. All that potential for good, for love, for memories that could have warmed the hearts of his children over the years. He knew he had lived only half a life.

Two Swords

Ty had failed to realize just how incredibly powerful his everyday actions and attitudes were in the lives of those in his home—until it was too late.

And, like Ty, the average man has that same power. He may not understand it. He may not choose to believe it. But it's a power deep and wide and high enough to influence and change human lives.

It's the power to send strong sons and clear-eyed, confident daughters into the world to right wrongs, fight worthy battles, and build strong families of their own.

It's a power that ripples outward for generations. Think of it! This power can positively affect our "children's children." What we do *today* in our homes can have a ripple effect on our great-great-grandchildren!

It can change a family tree forever.

In time, it can move a nation.

That's what it *could* do. But for so many men ruling their homes with an iron fist, that's not what's happening. Yes, the power is there. And yes, it's changing lives and affecting generations to come. But in many families, it's a power that destroys. And most men don't even realize that such power covers them.

Men, whether you realize it or not, you own two "swords" that are actually two forms of power. The handle of one gleams silver-blue, as though chiseled from a block of ice. You acquired the silver-handled sword early in your manhood, and you have continued to use it down through the years. You obtained it through sweat and grit and long, weary hours of labor. It's the sword you use most often in your job, and it remains your constant sense of protection, an equalizer in a rough-and-tumble world.

But you have a second sword as well. Its handle is burnished gold. This sword has been yours since birth, part of your inheritance, your birthright. You often leave it where it has been as long as you can remember—mounted over the fireplace. Something you may hardly notice. Something to dust twice a year. Most of the men you know in the work-a-day world want to wield the *silver*-handled sword. So do you. From the moment you completed your training in its use, it has been your deepest, most fervent desire to brandish that sword with all the strength, cunning, and endurance you can pull out of yourself.

For what purpose? To be regarded one day as a "Master of the Silver-Handled Sword"?

Yet, it's curious. The sword that looks so impressive in the marketplace seems a heavy, awkward thing when you walk through your front door in the evening. It can catch on the screen door, or even knock over the umbrella stand and a vase or two.

For that matter, you've found it extremely difficult to use the thing at home. You've tried to swing it around according to your training, but it causes your sons to wince and drives your daughters away.

You stand by the hearth and contemplate these strange things when suddenly, you find yourself gazing at a reflection of firelight in the molten gold of the "ornamental sword" hanging over the mantel. How it catches and holds the light!

Your own father rarely used it, just like his father before him. It may have been months since you've seen one brandished. In your corner of the world, few of the sword handlers in the marketplace even speak of it.

But how beautiful it is! On a whim, you unhook it from its mountings and draw the sword from its finely tooled scabbard. Catching and holding the red flames of a cherrywood fire, it seems to glow with a life of its own.

What if there was a tool, you wonder, *that could draw my sons and daughters to me rather than thrust them away? What if it could bring gladness and laughter?*

What if that tool also served as a weapon strong enough to drive back the darkness, banish loneliness from beneath this roof, overwhelm harsh words, force back the fears of childhood, overcome bitterness, slay the insecurities of adolescence, and kindle courage and hope whenever it was raised.

You do hold such a tool. And you do have a chance to use it, as well as your silver sword, for either tremendous good or great evil.

Two Strengths

The silver-handled sword is a man's *positional power*. That's the clout, control, prestige, and authority that come to a man because of where he works or what he does. It's his job title (whether he works on the line or supervises from the catwalk), the number of academic degrees he has earned or the way other men respect the clear mark of a craftsman when he finishes a job.

Personal power, on the other hand—the gold-handled sword—may or may not be accompanied by an impressive title, an American Express gold card, or a Ph.D. It has more to do with *who a man is* than with where he works or what he does. When you speak of a man's personal power, you immediately think of words reflecting character, such as *warmth*, *sensitivity*, *dependability*, *determination*, *genuine compassion*, and *caring*. It's what a man is (for good or ill) on his day off in his blue jeans and stocking feet. It's who he is when no one else is looking.

Is it a matter of choosing between the two swords? Does it have to be one or the other?

Not at all. What we're talking about is a working knowledge of *both* positional and personal power. There are times when you'll have to be skillful with the silver sword in our work-a-day, competitive, difficult world. There were times when Jesus picked up the silver sword of His positional power: stilling the storm, casting out demons, and raising the dead. But more often than not, you see Him choosing the gold sword, as when he expressed His personal power in touching a leper, calling Zacchaeus to come down from a tree, or weeping unashamedly at the death of a friend.

There's great benefit in having two swords. But many men have focused for so long on the silver-handled sword that they've neglected the deeper, stronger, longer-lasting power of the gold sword.

We're calling men to pick up both weapons of warfare, for we're in a raging battle for the hearts of our families. But can a man really learn to be an expert with two weapons at once? The truth is, *he has to*. He has no choice—that is, if he wants to win the love of a child, the genuine affection of a wife, and a "Well done" from his God.

We want to encourage you in the fine art of mastering your gold sword—and seeing your relationships improve greatly as a result.

And what happens when we do make the extra effort to pick up a sword that may not be natural for us? Whenever a man chooses to let the warmth of his gold sword radiate through his home, *it triples in power*. It opens eyes. Pulls back shades. Causes a stir. In some instances, it is virtually unforgettable.

I (John) remember playing my heart out for a high school football coach who rarely (I actually thought never!) used his gold sword to encourage or praise. It was late in a game we were supposed to win, but we were losing. And while I thought I had played a good game, in the fourth quarter I was pulled out after making a tackle.

Here it comes! I thought to myself as I jogged up to the coach. As the captain of the defense, I was going to get blasted for losing the game. But that's not what happened.

"John," he told me, "I just want you to know that I wish I had 10 more of you out on the field. I'm proud of how you're playing today. Now get back in the game!"

It has been more than 20 years since I nearly fell down after hearing those words. I remember floating back onto the field and playing even harder than before. We lost the game, but I won something that never showed up on the scoreboard—a crystal-clear picture in my mind. I had the memory of a silver sword expert who picked up the gold sword one time—and made four years of effort seem worthwhile.

Men tend to remember for decades specific words of encouragement their fathers spoke to them. When a man makes an effort to pick up the gold sword and use it under God's control, the world takes note. And the more we pick it up, the more we will shape those who love us and look to us to help define their lives.

Scripture encourages us to be strategic in the use of our words. When we speak, let's make our words count for something! Let's use words that build and encourage, rather than tear down or demean.

As the apostle Paul said in Ephesians 4: "Do not let any unwholesome talk come out of your mouths, but only what is helpful for building others up according to their needs, that it may benefit those who listen."

❧ ❧ ❧

How to Make Your Words Count

How can your words be like gold? Here are some suggestions:
- A timely compliment to a discouraged mate.
- A firm but loving word of warning to a wandering adolescent.
- A big heaping of praise to a child who is trying very hard to please you.
- An upbeat, confident appraisal of a situation when "the facts" are frowning another message.
- Words of trust in the Lord God.
- The words "I love you" anytime.

❧ ❧ ❧

The Silver Sword: Cutting into a Child's Heart

A child's heart is easily bruised. Easily broken. And once seriously damaged, no team of surgeons can repair it. Only the Almighty Himself has the skill to restore its original balance, potential, and capacities.

Recently, a 40-year-old man described a Saturday morning 28 years before that nearly stopped his heart—and is still affecting him today!

"I was just 12 when my Boy Scout troop planned a father-son camp-out," he said. "I was thrilled and could hardy wait to rush home and give my dad all the information. I wanted so much to show him all I'd learned in scouting, and I was so proud when he said he'd go with me.

"The Friday of the camp-out finally came, and I had all my gear out on the porch, ready to stuff it in his car the moment he arrived. We were to meet at the local school at 5:00 and carpool to the camp-ground. But Dad didn't get home until 7:00 P.M.

"I was frantic, but he explained how things had gone wrong at work and told me not to worry. We could still get up first thing in the morning and join the others. After all, we had a map. I was disappointed, of course, but I decided to make the best of it.

"First thing in the morning, I was up and had everything in his car while it was still getting light, all ready for us to catch up with my friends and their fathers at the campground. He had said we'd leave around 7 A.M., but he didn't get up until 9:30.

"When he saw me standing out front with the camping gear, he finally explained that he had a bad back and couldn't sleep on the ground. He hoped I'd understand and that I'd be a 'big boy' about it . . . but could I please get my things out of his car? He had several commitments he had to keep.

"Just about the hardest thing I've ever done was to go to the car and take out my sleeping bag, cooking stove, pup tent, and supplies. And then—while I was putting my stuff away and he thought I was out of sight—I watched my father walk out to the garage, sling his golf clubs over his shoulder, throw them into the trunk and drive away to keep his 'commitment.'

"That's when I realized my dad never meant to go with me to the camp-out. He just didn't have the guts to tell me."

How do you recalibrate a child's heart after it has been damaged by a dad's broken promise?

❧ ❧ ❧
Tools for Forging Your Own Gold Sword

After you've taken inventory of where you are, what negative effects you may have had on your spouse, children, and friends, look carefully at the future you want to have. Here are several steps to help you achieve that brighter future:

• *Honor your loved ones.* The most important ingredient in a successful family is placing high value on one another. When we decide someone is valuable, that's a major step in acting out our love for the person.

Honoring those in our homes means making a decision that they're heavyweights, worthy of great importance and appreciation.

• *Develop meaningful communication.* As we've interviewed successful families across the country, most say they need about an hour of real conversation sprinkled throughout each day. Perhaps it's five minutes in the morning, a 10-minute phone call from work, 20 minutes at dinner, and another 25 minutes carved out of the evening to provide this much-needed aspect of intimacy.

• *Deal with anger in a timely, healthy way.* In close-knit relationships, friction is inevitable. Often, that anger comes out of a blocked goal, an unmet expectation, or as a fear-based response. Other times, it comes out of a rightful sense of reaction to wrong.

Usually, by genuinely seeking to understand what happened, admitting when we're wrong, and specifically asking for forgiveness, we can see anger drain away. But if anger continues to reside in your heart or that of your loved one, don't assume it will simply get better over time. Talk it through.

• *Exhibit meaningful touching.* Meaningful, non-sexual touching is an important way of expressing warmth and security to a loved one. It puts actions to our words of affection and both physically and emotionally blesses those who are touched.

• *Provide regular emotional bonding experiences.* Genuine friendship comes from doing something more than just sitting around talking about friendship. Emotional bonding comes in the hundreds of "little" things we do with another person and usually become the biggest factors in building a satisfying relationship. Yes, it takes effort to carve out time to play together, exercise together, enjoy each other, and laugh with each other. But the closeness that results is worth it.

- *Practice financial stewardship.* One clear aspect of honoring our loved ones is providing security for them. While many things can add to the security a spouse or child feels, one major source of insecurity is financial irresponsibility. Work hard to stay out of debt (including that which is incurred by credit cards). The emotional and financial freedom it brings makes it that much easier to concentrate on carrying the gold sword.

This chapter is adapted from Gary Smalley and John Trent's latest book *The Hidden Value of a Man.* Smalley and Trent, authors of *The Language of Love* and *The Two Sides of Love,* are partners in Today's Family, a marriage and counseling ministry based in Phoenix.

What to Do When Kids Drive You Crazy

James C. Dobson, Ph.D.

*I*t will come as no surprise to parents, I'm sure, that children can be quite gifted at power games. These contests begin in earnest when children are between 12 and 15 months of age. Some get started even earlier. If you've ever watched a very young child continue to reach for an electric plug or television knob while his mother shouts, "No!" you've seen an early power game in progress.

It is probably not a conscious process at this stage, but later it will be. I'm convinced that a strong-willed child of three or older is inclined to challenge his mom and dad whenever he believes he can win. He will carefully choose the weapons and select the turf on which the contest will be staged. I've called these arenas "the battlefields of childhood." Let's look at some of the Gettysburgs, Stalingrads, and Waterloos that have gone down in family history.

Bedtime

One of the earliest contests begins at 18 months and one day—give or take a few hours. At precisely that time, a toddler who has gone to bed without complaining since he was born will suddenly say, "I'm not getting back in that crib again for as long as I live."

That is the opening salvo in what may be a five-year battle. It happens so quickly and unexpectedly that parents may be fooled by it. They will check for teething problems, a low-grade fever, or some other discomfort. "Why *now?*" they ask. I don't know. It just suddenly occurs to toddlers that they don't want to go to bed anymore, and they will fight it tooth and nail.

Although the tactics change a bit, bedtime will continue to be a battlefield for years to come. Any creative 6-year-old can delay going to bed for at least 45 minutes by an energetic and well-conceived system of stalling devices. By the time his mother gets his pajamas on, brings him six glasses of water, takes him to the bathroom twice, helps him say his prayers, and then scolds him for wandering out of his bedroom a time or two, she is thoroughly exhausted. It happens night after night.

A college friend of mine named Jim found himself going through this bedtime exercise every evening with his five-year-old son, Paulie. Jim recognized the tactics as a game and decided he didn't want to play anymore.

He sat down with his son that evening and said, "Now, Paulie, things are going to be different tonight. I'm going to get you dressed for bed; you can have a drink of water, and then we'll pray together. When that is done, I'm walking out the door, and I don't intend to come back. Don't call me again. I don't want to hear a peep from you until morning. Do you understand?"

Paulie said, "Yes, Daddy."

When the chores and prayers were completed, final hugs were

exchanged, and the lights were turned out. Jim told his son good night and left the room. Sweet silence prevailed in the house. But not for long. In about five minutes, Paulie called his father and asked for another drink of water.

"No way, Paulie," said his dad. "Don't you remember what I said? Now go to sleep."

After several minutes, Paulie appealed again for a glass of water. Jim was more irritated this time. He spoke sharply and advised his son to forget it. But the boy would not be put off. He waited for a few minutes and then re-opened the case. Every time Paulie called his dad, Jim became more irritated. Finally, he said, "If you ask for water one more time I'm going to come in there and spank you!"

That quieted the boy for about five minutes, and then he said, "Daddy, when you come in here to spank me would you bring me a glass of water please?"

The kid got the water. He did not get the spanking.

One of the ways of enticing children (perhaps ages four to eight) to go to bed is by the use of fantasy. For example, I told my son and daughter about "Mrs. White's Party" when they were little. Mrs. White was an imaginary lady who threw the most fantastic celebrations in the middle of the night. She ran an amusement park that made Disneyland boring by comparison.

Whatever was of interest to the children was worked into her repertoire—dogs, cats, sweets of all varieties, water slides, cartoons, thrilling rides, and anything else that excited Danae and Ryan's imaginations. Of course, the *only* way they could go to Mrs. White's party was to be asleep. No one who was awake would ever get an invitation.

It was fun to watch our son and daughter jump into bed and concentrate to go to sleep. Though it never happened, I wish I could have generated such interest that they would have actually dreamed about Mrs. White. Usually, the matter was forgotten the next morning.

By hook or crook, you must win the bedtime battle. The health of your child (and maybe your own) is at stake.

Food

The dinner table is another major battlefield of childhood, but it should be avoided. I have strongly advised parents not to get suckered into this arena. It is an ambush. A general always wants to engage the other army in a place where he can win, and mealtime is a lost cause.

A mother who puts four green beans on a fork and resolves to sit there until the child eats them is in a powerless position. The child can outlast her. And because meals come around three times a day, he will eventually prevail.

Instead of begging, pleading, bribing, and threatening a child, I recommend that good foods be placed before him cheerfully. If he chooses not to eat, then smile and send him on his way. He'll be back.

When he returns, take the same food out of the refrigerator, heat it, and set it before him again. Sooner or later, he will get hungry enough to eat. Do not permit snacking or substituting sweets for nutritious foods. But also do not fear the physical effects of hunger. A child will not starve in the presence of good things to eat. There is a gnawing feeling inside that changes one's attitude from "Yuck!" to "Yum!" usually within a few hours.

Schoolwork

Perhaps there is *no* greater source of conflict between generations today than schoolwork, and especially that portion assigned to be done at home. This is another battlefield where all the advantages fall to the youngster.

Only he knows for sure what was assigned and how the work is supposed to be done. The difficult child will capitalize on this information gap between home and school, claiming that "I got it all done in school," or "I have nothing to do tonight."

He reminds me of the kid who brought home four F's and a C on his report card. When his dad asked him what he thought the problem was, he said, "I guess I've been concentrating too hard on one subject."

Parents should know that *most* students go through an academic valley sometime between sixth and ninth grades in school. Some will quit working altogether during this time. Others will merely decrease their output. Very few will remain completely unaffected.

The reason is the massive assault made on adolescent senses by the growing-up process. Self-confidence is shaken to its foundation. Happy hormones crank into action, and sex takes over center stage. Who can think about school with all that going on? Or better yet, who wants to? As parents, you should watch for this diversion and not be dismayed when it comes.

Vacations and Special Days

Tell me why it is that children are the most obnoxious and irritating on vacations and during other times when we are specifically trying to please them? By all that is fair and just, you would expect them to think, "Boy! Mom and Dad are really doing something nice for us. They are taking us on this expensive vacation when they could have spent the money on themselves. And Dad would probably have preferred to go fishing (that's true) or do something else he wanted. But they care about us and have included us in their plans. Wow! I'm going to be as nice and as cooperative as possible. I'll try to get along with my sister, and I won't make any unusual demands. What a fun trip this will be!"

Do kids think that way? Fat chance! There is no such thing as intergenerational gratitude.

Before the family has even left town, the troops are fighting over who gets to sit by the window and which one will hold the dog. Little Sister yells, "I'm telling!" every few minutes.

Tensions are also building in the front seat. By the time they get to Phoenix, Dad is ready to blow his cork. It was tough enough for him to complete his office work and pack the car. But this bickering is about to drive him crazy. For 400 miles, he has endured arguments, taunts, jabs, pinches, tears, tattling, and unscheduled bathroom breaks.

Now he's starting to lose control. Twice he swings wildly at writhing bodies in the back seat. He misses and hurts his shoulder. He's driving faster by this time, but he's quit talking. The only clues to what he's feeling are his bloodshot eyes and the occasional twitch in his left cheek. Happy vacation, Pop. You have 13 days to go.

I once received a letter from a mother who had just returned from a stressful vacation similar to the one I described. For days, their two sons had whined and complained, insulting and fighting with each other. They kicked the back of their father's seat for hours at a time.

Finally, his fuse burned down to the dry powder. He pulled the car over to the side of the road and jerked the boys outside. Judgment Day had arrived.

After spanking them both, he shoved them back into the car and warned them to keep their mouths shut. "If I hear a peep from either of you for 30 minutes," he warned, "I'll give you some more of what you just had!"

The boys got the message. They remained mute for 30 minutes, after which the older lad said, "Is it all right to talk now?"

The father said sternly, "Yes. What do you want to say?"

"Well," continued the boy, "when you spanked us back there, my shoe fell off. We left it in the road."

It was the only good pair of shoes the kid owned. This time Mom went berserk and flailed at the back seat like a crazy lady. So ended another great day of family togetherness.

Is this the way parents should deal with a period of irritation from their children? Of course not, but let's face it. Parents are people. They have their vulnerabilities and flash points, too. The children should have been separated or perhaps offered spankings much earlier in the journey.

It is when parents are desperately trying to avoid punishment that their level of irritation reaches a dangerous level. By then, anything can happen. That is why I have contended that those who oppose corporal punishment on the grounds that it leads to child abuse are wrong. By stripping parents of the ability to handle frustrating behavior at an early stage, they actually increase the possibility that harm will be done to children as tempers rise.

Before we leave the matter of family vacations, let's deal with why it is that children seem to become more obnoxious on those special days. There are two good reasons for it. First, adults and children alike tend to get on each other's nerves when they are cooped up together for extended periods of time. But also, a difficult child apparently feels compelled to reexamine the boundaries whenever he thinks they may have moved.

This was certainly true of our children. On days when we planned trips to Disneyland, ski trips, or other holidays, we could count on them to become testy. It was as though they were obligated to ask, "Since this is a special day, what are the rules now?"

We would sometimes have to punish or scold them during times when we were specifically trying to build relationships. Perhaps that's why Erma Bombeck said, "The family that plays together gets on one another's nerves."

The Ramifications of Power

To repeat our thesis, these trouble spots between generations are not simply matters of differing opinion. If the conflicts amounted to no more than that, then negotiation and compromise would resolve them very quickly. Instead, they represent staging areas where the authority of the parent can be challenged and undermined.

The question being asked is not so much "Can I have my way?" as it is "Who's in charge here?" (Remember, now, that I'm describing the motivation of very strong-willed children. The compliant child is more subtle in his maneuvers for power.)

With the passage of time, the battles do tend to become more intense. What began as relatively minor struggles over bedtime or homework can develop into the most terrible conflicts. Some teenagers put their parents through hell on earth. Deep, searing wounds are inflicted that may never fully heal. For now, however, I want to conclude this discussion by explaining the great significance of power and its ramifications for parents.

The sense of power that is so attractive to children and to the rest of humanity is actually a very dangerous thing. Men have deceived, exploited, and killed to get it. Those who have achieved it have often been destroyed in its grasp. Lord Acton said, "Power corrupts, and absolute power corrupts absolutely." History has proved him right.

If power can be destructive to mature adults who think they know how to handle it, imagine what it will do to a mere child.

One of the characteristics of those who acquire power very early is a prevailing attitude of disrespect for authority. It extends to teachers, ministers, policemen, judges, and even to God Himself. Such an individual has never yielded to parental leadership at home. Why should he submit himself to anyone else? For a rebellious teenager, it is only a short step from there to drug abuse, sexual experimentation, running away, and so on. The early acquisition of power has claimed countless young victims by this very process.

What do we recommend, then? Should parents retain every vestige of power for as long as possible? No! Even with its risks, self-determination is a basic human right, and we must grant it systematically to our children. To withhold that liberty too long is to incite wars of revolution.

My good friend, Jay Kesler, observed that Mother England made that specific mistake with her children in the American colonies. They grew to become rebellious "teenagers" who demanded their freedom. Still, she refused to release them, and unnecessary bloodshed ensued. Fortunately, England learned a valuable lesson from that painful experience. Some 171 years later, she granted a peaceful and orderly transfer of power to another tempestuous offspring named India. Revolution was averted.

This, then, is our goal as parents: we must not transfer power too early, even if our children take us daily to the battlefield. Mothers who make that mistake are some of the most frustrated people on the face of the earth.

On the other hand, we must not retain parental power too long, either. Control will be torn from our grasp if we refuse to surrender it voluntarily. The granting of self-determination should be matched stride for stride with the arrival of maturity, culminating with complete release during early adulthood.

Sounds easy, doesn't it? We all know better. I consider this orderly transfer of power to be one of the most delicate and difficult responsibilities in the entire realm of parenthood.

4

Let's Go Home Again

Gary L. Bauer

*H*oney, I love you. Tell the kids to study hard."

In isolation these are not extraordinary words. But they took on special meaning when they were spoken on nationwide television in a moment of high stress.

In the early days of the 1991 Gulf War, the Iraqi leadership heartlessly paraded captured pilots on that country's government-run network.

My heart broke for these men as my family and I, secure in our own home, watched the drama unfold on the screen. One captured pilot in particular left a lasting impression on me. His face was swollen from injuries suffered in the aircraft crash as well as being pummeled by Saddam Hussein's thugs.

Fearing for his life, he followed the Iraqi script and unemotionally mumbled a few words of propaganda into the television camera. But then, he seized the chance to add those otherwise mundane words: "Honey, I love you. Tell the kids to study hard."

In four short words a husband assured a waiting wife that no matter how many miles separated them, and no matter what danger threatened him, his love for her was the first priority in his mind. In six more words the children were reminded that they still had a dad, that he wanted them to work hard, to achieve the most they could. It was a dramatic display of the love of a father and a testament to the power of heart and home.

Ever since then, whenever I have an opportunity, I share this moving episode with audiences across the country. The reaction is always the same. The room usually grows still; tears fall here and there; husbands and wives reach for each other's hands. For most of us the values expressed by that captured POW are the values that motivate and give meaning to our day-to-day lives. These are the reasons we get up in the morning to tackle another day. These are the reasons we work hard, save, sacrifice, and when it doesn't seem possible to go on—we do it all over again. These are the ties that bind.

I have worked in Washington, D.C., for most of my adult life trying to bring some common sense to the laws our government passes. But for most Americans, thankfully, life doesn't revolve around the latest legislation passed by Congress or the most recent double-talk uttered by some high-level bureaucrat.

For most of us, even after years of hearing traditional values ridiculed, life is still helping hands and good neighbors. It is lovingly packed lunch boxes, night-time prayers, dinners well talked over, hard work, and a little put away for the future. No government can ever command these things, and no government can ever duplicate them. They are done out of love and a commitment to the future.

That pilot eventually came safely home. I am sure he was sustained in his captivity by faith and the strong family bonds that normally hold us together. I believe millions of other Americans have endured their own form of captivity in recent years. We have been held hostage by a culture that mocks family values. We have seen our most deeply held beliefs ridiculed by sophisticates who disdain these values simply because they are held by common men and women. We have been subjected to assaults on the reliable standards of right and wrong we try to teach our children. Now, like that POW, we are ready to go home.

"I'm going home." There may be sweeter phrases in the English language—"I love you," for example—but few phrases pack as much emotional wallop as the simple expression of returning to the place of one's birth, or to the haven of a house well lived in.

All of us experience homecomings during our lifetime. Some are grand and nostalgic, as when we return to the streets where we first rode a bike, or the neighborhood where we made the best friends we ever had. Others are bittersweet because someone we loved is gone, or something—maybe everything—is changed. Other homecomings are as routine as pulling into your driveway after a hard day at the office.

Marks on the Door, Stains on the Floor

I remember at 10 years of age running home, late for dinner after a sandlot ball game that went too long. What a sight that old house was with my father's car parked in front signaling he was home from work.

I remember the sound the old iron gate made as I pushed through it. My mouth still waters as I recall the smell of a meat-and-potato dinner drifting down through the window. The kind of dinner that (in those days before cholesterol-counting became necessary) was always followed by deep-dish apple pie and ice cream.

I remember coming home another day, from high school, when President Kennedy was assassinated. I remember the long walk home and passing the town post office, its flag already at half-staff. Like everyone else I felt a sense of panic and loss unlike anything I had ever experienced.

But somehow the sight of that solid red brick house and the knowledge that my mother waited inside were enough to reassure a confused teenaged boy, more than any TV commentator could, that we would weather this crisis, too.

In a few years there would be weekend trips, my car loaded down with dirty laundry as I sought relief from the rigors of college and weeks of being really away from home for the first time. Today, when I take my family back to the home where I grew up, a million memories flood my mind: The marks on the kitchen door to record how tall I was; the stain on the hardwood floor where a chemistry experiment conducted by a budding 12-year-old scientist went awry; the BB still embedded in my bedroom wall when I learned all guns are loaded.

My children love to go to the third floor of the old house to rummage through the boxes. There in the cartons is the evidence of the life and times of their grandfather, "Pop," as well as of their father. A faded football letter provides an opportunity to tell them about the game where my father scored three touchdowns in shoes three sizes too big. (Or was it two touchdowns in shoes two sizes too big? Time grows all tales.) A picture of a graduation class from Marine Corps boot camp is scanned. "There's Pop!" shouts Sarah, third row up on the end, taken just days before the men were sent into battle.

The children sit spellbound listening to the stories of heroism and valor that my father told me late at night, often with tears in his eyes, and that I now pass on to them. How can I possibly make them understand the extraordinary feats done by ordinary men and women to preserve our liberty?

Sarah excitedly thumbs through a second-grade workbook with my name printed in an unsure hand in the front. She counts the number of tests with "100" on them but seems to find more comfort from the occasional "C." Perhaps the papers are reassuring to her. They let her know that you can still make something of yourself, even if you are not perfect.

I tell them about teachers who made a difference in my life, even when I didn't realize it at the time; about how painfully shy their father once was (and still is), head down in the last row in hope he wouldn't be called upon. (My first-grade teacher wrote to my parents, "Gary must overcome his reluctance to talk." I did, much to the chagrin of my critics.)

My son, Zachary, listens wide-eyed as I tell him of schoolyard bullies—of the times I stood my ground and other times I ran away from a guy named "Slugger," hoping somehow in these stories Zachary will learn something that will help him, as a man, come to grips with fear and honor, bravery and courage.

They learn, again, that I am not perfect, that their parents' before them had victories and defeats, that we did good and made mistakes, that we sometimes loved and lost and sometimes loved and won. They learn about faith. Each of them begs for and receives one of the childhood Bibles, the pages turning yellow and the covers coming unglued. They love the gold stars pasted on the inside, each one for a verse memorized.

There is a box in the attic back in our present home in Virginia, too. As each year passes, it fills with memories and momentoes. Someday, I suppose my children will take my grandchildren on a treasure hunt through those relics of my life and their childhood. They will find the stacks of letters my parents sent me, letters of love and encouragement through days of doubt in law school, or when I was struggling to find that first job.

Maybe they will laugh when they discover their school papers and wonder at those years when reciting the alphabet and counting to 100 were the most important things in life. There will be a lot of certificates in the box, awards and commissions from my years in government. And photos, too, at the White House with the president or in the Cabinet Room.

I guess my grandchildren will be suitably impressed. But when my time has come and gone, I hope my children will tell their own that they remember me most cheering at a Little League game, playing in the yard, leading a mealtime prayer, or taking a quiet walk. Or perhaps they will recall some bit of wisdom I was able to pass on or the love their mother, Carol, and I have had for each other.

I used to be impatient with my parents when they wanted me to stand still long enough to take a picture of a new suit or when I got into my car with all my earthly possessions in the back seat, to drive to Washington, D.C. Now I treasure those snapshots that remind me who I was and where I was going.

Belated Awakening

Homecomings can be humbling. Many of us leave home convinced we are going to conquer the world. We are anxious to shuck off the restraints of family and traditions, to cut our own swath and make our own rules.

At 18 we know we can do it better, make it faster, and see it all. Somewhere along the way we learn we didn't know quite as much as we thought. Our ideas weren't as new as we took them to be. Suddenly the "quaint" homespun wisdom that once was rejected takes on new life. The first trip home after such an awakening is a return to reality.

Could it be that America needs humbly to "go home"? For over 30 years now we have tossed off many of the rules and restraints painfully learned by trial and error through thousands of years of civilization. Thinking we could have it all and do it all, we went on the equivalent of a national binge. Instead of self-sacrifice, our culture has elevated self-fulfillment as the theme of the hour.

Responsibility has been de-emphasized, while at the same time we have created whole new categories of rights—usually rights to some form of self-destructive behavior. Virtue was put on the shelf and blushing became passé. Faced with an epidemic of venereal disease, our cultural gurus, from Hollywood to the sports halls, urge us to worship at the altar of "safe sex."

Now we've awakened with a monster hangover. Nearly 30 percent of our children are born out of wedlock. Family breakup is at record levels. Taxes are high, but government wants even more revenue. The federal budget deficit is out of sight. The streets aren't safe. In some of our gunfire-wracked cities, even the bassinets aren't safe. We have less time with our families. Even with all the extra hours we spend in the labor force, we are falling behind competitively.

If ever there were a time to go home, this is it.

Some pessimists argue that going home, after this many years, is impossible. We've been away too long, they say. The old house is boarded up, and the folks have moved away and left no forwarding address.

Others believe there's no need to call it a night. "The party's still going strong," they say. "Things are just fine."

I believe both are wrong. It is possible for us to rediscover our roots and reclaim the best in our history. It is desirable for our people to pull back from disaster and rededicate ourselves to hearth and home.

In fact, millions of Americans never left home! Despite all that has happened in the last 30 years, most Americans have resisted decay in the popular culture. Millions of others are rethinking the lifestyles of the '70s and '80s and finding them unsatisfactory. A counterrevolution is beginning.

Hearth, Home, and Heartland

Signs abound that Americans are indeed "going home." In area after area, from the renewal of religious faith to rejection of radical feminism's extreme agenda, to discontent with the ravages of divorce and promiscuity, the first stirrings of a rebirth of family values are being felt.

The signs exist in dozens upon dozens of personal stories, in data tables and graphs, in the refusal of millions of Americans to accept the idea that at our nation is too "modern" to care about so backward an institution as the family.

The love of hearth and home knows no social or economic limits. Home is where the heart is, whether it's in a fashionable suburb or an inner-city flat.

In fact, it is often in the homes of those with the fewest possessions that the biggest hearts are found. Queen Elizabeth learned this first-hand during her 1991 trip to the United States, when she visited the home of 67-year-old Alice Frazier in one of the toughest drug-ridden neighborhoods of Southeast Washington.

As the entourage of dignitaries entered her home, Mrs. Frazier—

obviously not steeped in royal protocol—did what she usually does when a guest crosses her threshold: She rushed forward and hugged a startled and befuddled Queen Elizabeth.

The picture appeared the next day on the front page of *The Washington Post*. I don't know what the reaction of our English cousins was, but the event warmed the hearts of most Americans I talked to. Alice Frazier was obviously proud of her modest home, filled with the aroma of fried chicken and potato salad.

It was a public housing unit that she had been able to buy under an innovative program that allows low-income public-housing residents to take over their apartments. It was her home, and as such it was every bit a castle. There are Alice Fraziers all over America—good and decent people who make houses into castles. They are the backbone of the nation, and they deserve better than they get.

The Possible Dream

Research shows Americans are rediscovering the importance of family values. Over 93 percent of us now say that a good family life is "very important." The increase is particularly strong among young people. *U.S. News & World Report* recently found that "two-thirds of . . . voters agree on a set of core conservative values by which to govern society, starting with a belief in the family as the basic social unit, less government, lower taxes and the need for more religion." We are hungry for safe, sane lives, strong families, love, commitment, and values.

Despite our problems, most Americans still believe in the same solid values about which we have always cared. In fact, millions of Americans—of all races and economic backgrounds—have resisted cultural pressures and have built strong, stable families. Americans are ready for a rebirth of the values and commitments that have served us so well in the past and that hold the only hope for a future that works.

I confess to the same optimism. There are reasons for hope. Our problems, while serious, are not as severe as our negative media would lead us to believe. We have economic troubles, but we have lived through depression. We have internal strife, but we have lived through civil war and global strife. Most of America's families are pulling through. Most households cling together. Most young people aspire to productive, independent lives. Most young adults, upright and responsible, hope to build families of their own. Most families endure.

After 30 years of "experimentation" in which old values were tossed overboard, there is a great yearning among our people to return "home." We are looking for someone to show us the way. I believe the weakened bonds between husbands and wives and between parents and children can be strengthened again. I believe our neighborhoods can be made safe and our schools can transmit reliable standards of right and wrong. I believe we are capable of teaching our children about virtue, love, and faith. I believe we can come up with a better way to deal with an unwanted pregnancy than abortion. I believe the racial division can be healed and our family life renewed.

We hunger to know that our lives matter. We want affirmation that home and family are important and that the values of the past are still relevant today. We want to go home. We should begin that trip now, while we still remember the way.

Gary Bauer is president of the Family Research Council in Washington, D.C. Taken from *Our Journey Home*, by Gary Bauer. Copyright © 1992. Word Publishing, Dallas, Texas 75234. All rights reserved.

5

Mom, You're Incredible!

Linda Weber

O ver the years, it seems some of our common sense for mothering has been lost. Maybe it's because so many young mothers no longer enjoy the proximity of extended family, where skills and insight are passed from older moms to younger ones. Maybe it's because before we have kids, we think that knowing how to be a good mother and having the right answers just come naturally. But we soon learn better.

A *lot* is expected of moms today. Well-adjusted kids don't just happen. Developing their hearts and spirits must be the main thing, the central focus of our efforts. As the German proverb says, "The main thing is to make the main thing always remain the main thing."

Well-adjusted kids come from families in which mothering is seen as a complex, beautiful challenge worthy of everything Mom can give to it. Mothering shapes lives and attitudes, one way or another.

The truth is, motherhood can't be discounted. That's why I'm concerned as I see more moms fitting work outside the home into their schedules and having to deal with the issue of child care.

I know I'm stepping into dangerous territory by talking about child care. My friends at Focus on the Family tell me that whenever they air a broadcast or publish an article about working mothers, regardless of what they say, they get critical letters from both sides of the issue.

Moms who work outside the home write, "Why are you trying to make us feel more guilty?" Stay-at-home moms write, "Why are you downplaying the importance of what we do?" It seems to be a real Catch-22 subject.

Nonetheless, because I know you love your children deeply and want to be the best mom you can possibly be, and because I want to be a friend who helps you toward that goal, I'm going to venture boldly into this arena and say what I believe with all my heart.

I know there are many moms who have children still at home and who truly have no choice but to work outside the home. For them, it isn't just a matter of wanting to maintain a certain lifestyle. Even in those cases, however, as in all others, a mother's care is the preferred choice. I don't say that to make anyone feel guilty; it's just a fact.

Even if you have no choice but to work outside the home and leave your children in day care, please stay with me because I will offer some suggestions for finding the very best care available to you.

The Search Begins

For some reason, telephone poles seem to have become billboards around our community. I can stop at almost any intersection and read a number of flyers.

> Garage Sale, 8 to 2, Sat. only
> Firewood, Maple & Fir, Delivered
> Reward: Have You Seen Our Golden Retriever?
> Quality Child Care in My Home

Quality child care? From a phone number stapled to a telephone pole along Hogan Road? Is that all the recommendation needed today to consider placing children in a stranger's care? Have we become so desperate? Is child care really that much in demand?

Not long ago, I received a letter from Kendall, a young friend who works in a day-care center. It read:

> Working at a day-care center for the past three years has given me a stark view of where families, especially women, are headed. Motherhood is no longer valued, and it is seen more as a mark of prestige than as the precious gift it truly is. Our little girls are growing up playing office, banker and travel agent while they take their baby dolls to a day-care center or sitter.

That was a strong statement, so I called Kendall and asked her to tell me more about her concerns. She replied, "Not all mothers who bring their children to day care are bad mothers. But I see a lot of tired women who don't have any patience at the end of the day. I see too many of them whisk their kids off to another baby-sitter for the evening while they take care of themselves."

When Kendall was little, she played house. There was a mommy and a daddy. "These little girls don't play house," she told me. "They never cook a meal; they microwave everything. I never see them nurturing their dolls. They just put them in a crib and have their friends take care of them. These little girls all want to be like boys. I see that a lot. They're very competitive, but they're not at all nurturing."

Kendall works in a day-care center because she loves children. She has no ax to grind with day care and no grudge to bear against mothers. She's merely reporting what she sees. And what she sees is too many mothers forgetting to nurture and using child care as a substitute parent. And she sees little girls mimicking their mommies—putting their baby dolls aside and going to the office.

What the Research Says

I shudder when I read what researchers are discovering as they study children placed in child care at early ages. This research doesn't point fingers at the abilities or intentions of child-care providers. Instead, it points fingers at the effects of parental absence. No matter how great the caregiver, the parent is needed most.

Brenda Hunter, writing in *Home by Choice*, said,

> Babies need their mothers. They need them during their earliest years, more than they need baby-sitters, toys, or the material comforts a second income will buy. The evidence since 1980 indicates that when a baby is placed in substitute care, even good quality care such as with a nanny, for 20 or more hours a week during his first year of life, he is at risk psychologically. If a mother returns to work during her baby's first year, there's a significant chance the child will be insecurely attached to its mother and/or father.

Freud describes the relationship of a young child to his mother as "unique, without parallel, established unalterably for a whole lifetime as the first and strongest love object and as the prototype of all later love relationships for both sexes."

If that relationship is interrupted by child care substituted for the mother, the impact is immense. British psychiatrist John Bowlby states, "The young child's hunger for his mother's love and presence is as great as his hunger for food. Her absence inevitably generates a powerful sense of loss and anger." Young children desperately need the emotional accessibility of a parent. That stability forms the foundation for all relationships to come.

Patterns Are Set

Child-care advocates will tell you a child naturally establishes strong bonds with a caregiver, and that's true. But that doesn't necessarily mean it's good. "A child's mind is like a videotape recorder, carefully transcribing every word, right down to the tone of voice and facial expressions," wrote author Richard Strauss. "And all of it contributes to the person he will become. Some psychologists say his emotional pattern is set by the time he is 2 years old."

Whom will your child pattern himself after? Whom will he see when he wakes? When he experiences the rushes of good feelings from being fed, changed, or bathed, who will be indelibly etched in his mind, you or a caregiver?

Others just don't have the deep concern for my children that I have. No one else is ready to make the sacrifices, to take the time to nurture and encourage as I am. So who could better care for my child, especially during his first years when he is so impressionable and easily molded?

Many people can carefully attend to your young child. Many people can provide quality food and supervision. But that doesn't ensure the emotional health, stability, or well-being of your little one. Mom, your child's identity will be indelibly stamped with the identity of the significant caregiver. His security and self-esteem will be permanently affected by his setting, especially if he has to establish himself in a crowd of other little folks all clamoring for attention, recognition, and regard.

You must look deeper than good food and supervision when you determine for yourself, "What is quality child care?"

Some Strategies

The bottom line is this: If you have to use child care, use it as a supplement to your nurturing, not a substitute. Treat your search for care with as much thoroughness as you would use in searching for the best heart surgeon. Use the following three guidelines in conducting your search.

First, *look for a home atmosphere*, with only one or two other children present, rather than a large-group setting such as a franchised day-care center. There's just no way kids can get the individualized attention they need in the large-group situation. The ideal situation might be to find someone who can come to your home and give your children the most secure environment of all.

Second, *do a thorough examination of all potential caregivers.* Interview them closely, ask for references, and question all the references as well. It's not a bad idea to ask local churches for recommendations, but that's not fool-proof, either. Examine those people as carefully as any others. And only consider people with a proven record of positive experiences.

Finally, look for caregiving situations that will allow you to *maximize your own involvement with your children.* Perhaps you can trade baby-sitting with a friend. Or you might find a job-sharing arrangement or a part-time position that meets your financial needs but doesn't require you to leave your children with someone else a full eight hours a day. Also explore the possibility of a home-based business if you have skills that can be used that way, such as word processing or craft making.

Mom, you have a unique place in your child's life, and you will make a unique impact—one way or the other. Make it the best that's within your power to give.

🌺 🌺 🌺
What in the World Does a Mom Do All Day?

Being a mom is a job with a capital J. We work our fingers to the bone, push our nerves to the edge, and use every skill possible to accomplish the demands of the day.

Just what does a mother do all day? Today's college student can't imagine. Numbers of women are baffled by what they'd do with "all that time" if they had to be home. Sometimes Mom herself can't remember.

Well, what am I? I'm the following:

- baby feeder, changer, bather, rocker, burper, hugger, and listener to crying and fussing and thousands of questions
- picker-upper of food and debris cast on the floor
- problem solver, determiner of action, and the one who gives those talks to whomever needs them
- phone messenger
- comforter, encourager, counselor
- hygienist

- linguistic expert for two-year-old dialects
- trainer of baby-sitters
- listener—for the husband as well as the children—about their day, their needs, their concerns, their aspirations
- teacher of everything from how to chew food to how to drive a car
- assistant on school projects
- questioner, prober to promote thinking
- censor of TV, movies, and books
- reader of thousands of children's books
- planner and hostess of children's birthday parties
- planner and hostess of adult dinner parties
- short-order cook for meals budding athletes depend upon
- central control for getting the appliance fixed or the carpet shampooed
- executioner of ants, roaches, wasps, and other pests
- resident historian in charge of photo albums, baby books, and school record books (at my house, I'm on book 50)
- resident encyclopedia source for all those hard questions
- defroster of the freezer
- food preservation expert
- family secretary, confirming dinner reservations, travel, and accommodations
- keeper and locator of birth certificates and other valuable documents
- ironer of wrinkles
- appointment desk for the family's visits to the doctor, the dentist, the orthodontist, the barber, and the mechanic
- one who prays
- cleaner of the oven, the drawers, the closets, the garage, the curtains, the bedding, the windows, and even the walls
- refinisher of furniture
- emergency medical technician and "ambulance" driver
- hubby's romantic, attentive spouse
- enjoyer of those moments when nothing is happening, no one is calling, nothing demands attention

And what are some things I do? Well, among many others, the following:

- clip ten fingernails and ten toenails for each young child regularly
- return library books
- get film developed
- choose gifts, purchase gifts, wrap gifts for birthdays, Christmas, Father's Day, Mother's Day, wedding showers, baby showers, and anniversaries
- mail packages, buy stamps
- drop off the dry cleaning; pick up the dry cleaning
- have pictures framed
- haul everything that needs repair
- attend recitals
- attend every school sporting event imaginable
- chauffeur everyone everywhere
- cover for my sick son on his 4 A.M. paper route
- comb a little girl's hairdo
- help in the classroom
- attend school PTA meetings and conferences
- act as a room mother, making things and organizing parties
- chaperon field trips and special events
- coordinate car pools (it makes men shudder)
- lead Scouts, Blue Birds, and a Sunday school class
- purchase most everything for the family and the home
- deliver forgotten lunches, forgotten homework, and forgotten athletic gear
- make bank deposits and withdrawals
- attend church, Bible studies, committee meetings, showers, weddings, choir practices, board meetings, potlucks, and neighborhood meetings just to "stay active and informed"

This article is adapted from a Focus on the Family book: *Mom, You're Incredible!* by Linda Weber, a mother of three strapping sons. She and her husband, Stu, live near Portland, Oregon.

6

When Kids Are Home Alone

Sandra Picklesimer Aldrich

Diane Jones will never forget the first time she left her four children home by themselves. She instructed Sarah, 12, Cary, nine, and Daniel, six, to be good and let their infant brother, Spencer, keep taking his nap. "I'll be back in 20 minutes," she said, as she rushed off to the local supermarket to buy milk and diapers.

But when she returned to her street, she drove up to every parent's nightmare: two fire trucks in the driveway, a paramedic ambulance on the front lawn, and two police cars at the curb!

The blood drained from her face. She struggled to catch her breath. How was she going to tell her husband she'd killed their children?

She hastily parked the car and jumped out. Hysterically, she ran toward the house, but a husky policeman grabbed her in a bear hug.

She struggled against his clasped arms, straining for the porch.

At that moment, Diane's three oldest children came thundering out of the house, sobbing.

"What happened to the baby?" Diane wailed.

"Nothing," Sarah managed. "He's still asleep."

Bewildered, Diane looked from child to child and realized they were crying only because she was crying. The policeman directed her attention to a downed electrical wire near the driveway. He hadn't been trying to keep her from going to the house—just away from the dangerous wire that had fallen while she was gone. A neighbor had spotted it and called the electrical company; hence, all the emergency equipment.

With her knees still trembling, Diane escorted the three children back into the house. She didn't leave them home alone for a *long* time.

New Questions

Most of us won't come home to a street filled with fire trucks and paramedic units, but we're afraid we might. Why? Because we've all heard reports of a sudden fire that claimed innocent lives in minutes.

Despite the dangers, leaving children home alone is a regular occurrence in millions of homes across the country. Some parents, as in Diane's case, have their children "baby-sit themselves" while they run a quick errand. Others feel their kids are old enough to be left unsupervised while they attend a PTO meeting or enjoy a "date-night" dinner. But for many two-income and single-parent families, their children come home from school to an empty house, where they do homework, watch TV, or wait until their mother or father arrives from work.

A few parents are more brazen. During Christmas 1992, while Kevin McAllister (Macaulay Culkin) was foiling bad guys in the hit movie *Home Alone 2*, David and Sharon Schoo of St. Charles, Illinois, were vacationing in Acapulco, Mexico. Back in Illinois, authorities discovered that their two children, Nicole, 10, and Diana, four, had been left behind for *nine days* while their parents were getting a tan.

Although the Schoos acted inappropriately—most would say stupidly—when *can* parents leave their children home alone? How old should they be? For how long? What rules should parents set?

I began to ask myself those same questions after my husband died 11 years ago. My son, Jay, was 10, and daughter, Holly, was eight. Suddenly, I didn't have a spouse to help look after the children, and during those turbulent times I *had* to leave my children home alone for short periods.

Based on my experiences and interviews with moms around the country, here are a few suggestions to make sure your children are safe at home when you're not there:

• First, *determine if your children are old enough.* Look at the maturity level of the child. Most mothers feel children under the age of 10 are too young to be left for more than 15 to 20 minutes—and only during the daytime. For evening hours, children should be older than 10.

Carol and her husband are the parents of an 11-year-old daughter and two boys, nine and seven, who all get along well. Recently, they started leaving the children for an hour or two in the early evening, but they are home early so the youngsters don't have to go to bed without supervision.

Carol has also made sure the children are familiar with getting out of the house in an emergency and how to call 911. She always writes down the phone numbers of the restaurant and several neighbors.

Barbara and her husband feel confident they can leave their three teenagers (16, 15, and 14) alone, but they still call them periodically. They also have a friend stop by occasionally to "borrow" something and check on them.

Rhonda started leaving her daughters when the oldest was 13 and the others were 11 and eight. She alerted the next-door neighbor that the children were alone, but she wanted them to learn responsibility at home before they were asked to baby-sit for other families.

A Kansas mother still remembers the trauma of having to leave her ill five-year-old in the care of her 10-year-old brother. The father was away, they had no extended family or nearby neighbors, and she would lose her job if she took time off. She felt she had no choice but to leave them alone—but well-armed with books and already prepared meals. The mother worried a great deal.

"I was afraid the house would burn down," she says. "I called several times to check on them. Even though that happened years ago, I still feel guilty about having left my sick little girl to be cared for by her brother."

Of course, *where* you live—an urban neighborhood, the suburbs, or in the country—will also color your decision on when your children are old enough to be home alone.

• *Check alternatives to the traditional "baby-sitter."* Most early teens are convinced they can handle being alone. This is where you may have to get creative. One single mother paid an older neighbor to go into her house each afternoon and start dinner just as the children arrived home from school. Since the woman was helping their mom, the children didn't think of her as a baby-sitter.

Other mothers hire a college student to assist the children with homework after school. Another creative mother arranged to have her 11-year-old daughter help with the preschoolers at their church day-care facility. The girl was able to spend time with the toddlers—an age group that she enjoyed—and the mother knew she was safe.

• *Set up definite rules—including those for chores and visitors.* Do you want their homework started immediately? Do you allow "wind-down" time with the TV first? May they call their friends? Whatever your rules are, make sure the children understand them.

One Midwestern mother, Allison, started leaving her children alone the summer they were 11 and 10 years old—and only as a test run for the school year. That fall, when they got off the school bus in front of their house, they walked directly inside—as per their mother's strict instructions—and started their homework. Allison usually arrived from her nursing duties an hour after they did. Among her rules were these: Under *no* circumstance were they to cook, answer the phone, or open the door.

Her children listened too well. The day came when Allison forgot her house key. She banged on the door, shouting that it was their mother. The children were upstairs, so they couldn't hear her voice. Then she went to the neighbors to call them. Into the third ring, she remembered the rule about not answering the phone. Allison's one hope was that the answering machine was still on. On the sixth ring, the machine picked up, allowing her to shout that it was okay to let Mom in. They heard her voice from their bedrooms and came downstairs to open the front door.

When my children were younger, a major rule was that they couldn't have visitors if I wasn't home. When we moved to Colorado in their late teens, that rule was bent occasionally—but only if the visitor was of the same gender and the other parent knew I wasn't home.

• *Make sure your children are secure and know who to call in an emergency.* Stress that they are never to open the door and are never to tell a stranger on the phone that they're alone.

Of course we don't want our children to lie, but they don't need to tell everything either. Thus, I always instructed my youngsters to say, "I'm sorry, but my mother can't come to the phone right now. If you'll leave a message, I'll have her call you back."

• *Talk to your children about their concerns.* Ask them what they dislike most about being home alone and work out ways to make it less painful.

For Jamie, it was coming into a dark house in the winter. His mother's simple investment in an electric timer for the lights took care of the problem. Many parents respect their children's feelings and won't leave them alone if they are afraid of the dark or are uncomfortable with younger brothers or sisters.

• *Make sure they have the phone number where you'll be.* But insist they don't call you to referee their squabbles.

Sharon remembers the tired mother in the fabric department who got a call right in the middle of cutting a length of material. Sharon could hear her pleading with first one son and then another, saying she'd help them settle it when she got home in a couple of hours.

Sharon confesses that her first thought was *Why doesn't she stay home with her kids where she belongs?* It was easy for Sharon to be self-righteous: Her husband paid her bills, and their children were cared for a few hours each day by a housekeeper.

But when her husband left her for another woman, Sharon's world came tumbling in. Eventually, she even had to take a job outside the home. Then she remembered the fabric worker with a new understanding.

• *If you're a working parent, seek out flex time.* When I took a nine-to-five job after my husband died, my work schedule suddenly thrust my children into the world of latchkey kids. I wasn't handling the trauma well at all, so I talked it over with my boss. He allowed me to "flex" my work schedule so I could start work an hour earlier. This meant I could arrive home only an hour after my children did.

By offering flex-time schedules to working moms, employers can help us be available to our family. The company, at the same time, benefits by gaining an employee with greatly improved morale.

• *Extend to your children the same respect you demand of them.* I have always expected my teens to let me know where they are, who they're with and what time they expect to be home. If any of those plans change, they are to call me. I, in turn, offer them the same courtesy.

However, I still remember one night when I goofed: Friends and I decided to stop for coffee after a special meeting at the church. The restaurant phone was out of order, and it was inconvenient to find another one. I figured both teens would be in bed anyway by then, so why bother them?

When I arrived home, 16-year-old Jay—who had sent his younger sister on to bed—was still up, supposedly doing homework. His stern "Where were you?" and "Well, you still could have called" not only echoed my own earlier lectures to him but let me know that my youngsters worry about me just as much as I worry about them.

• *Pray—a lot!* We can't follow our children through life, clearing their road of every potential hazard. Instead, we must do what we can to provide for their safety and then leave the rest to the heavenly Father. Be comforted by the fact that He loves our children even more than we do.

Home Alone—for a Minute

For Diane Jones, it was a year and a half before she had the courage to leave the children alone again. But one particular day she'd been especially busy with laundry, preparations for that night's church supper, and answering letters. Eighteen-month-old Spencer was studiously stacking his wooden blocks on the family room carpet while his 10-year-old brother, Daniel, read nearby. It was a perfect time to mail her letters at the corner mailbox before the five o'clock pickup.

She explained to Daniel that she was going to run down the street and would be back in just a couple of minutes. She left exact instructions that he was to watch his little brother's every move.

She quickly strode the half block, threw the letters into the mailbox and walked back home. As she opened the door, Daniel was frantic.

"Mom, I'm so sorry," he sobbed. "I didn't mean for it to happen. I took my eyes off Spencer for just a moment. . . ."

Diane gasped, "Oh, no!" and rushed past Daniel, expecting to find Spencer sprawled on the floor, dead.

Instead, the toddler was standing by the kitchen table with chocolate brownie smeared all over his face. He was enjoying the dessert she'd prepared for that evening's church supper.

Poor Diane. She knew she could never leave any of her children alone again—ever. At least not until they're married.

Some of this material is adapted from Sandra Aldrich's book *From One Single Mother to Another*. Copyright © 1991. Regal Books, Ventura, California 93003. Used by permission.

PART TWO

FOCUS ON YOUNG CHILDREN

7

Teaching Children to Work

Jean Lush

I'm often asked how important it is to teach children to work. I can answer that in one word: Very.

A few years ago, a state rehabilitation center asked me to treat men who were classified as unemployable. These men were not derelicts, but nicely dressed and well-spoken.

After six months of seeing these men, I found one common factor: None had learned to work while he was young. Each had a different reason; some of their families had been well-to-do, others were slightly handicapped and had never been required to work. Some grew up with no one around to care *whether* they worked or not.

But a surprising number had good, kind mothers who wanted their home to be a cushioned retreat. Some mothers actually told them, "You'll have plenty of time to work when you're older. I want you to have a happy childhood."

Little did these mothers know what they were saying. A happy childhood where nothing is required? That's a paradox. Children who have no responsibilities tend to quarrel *more* than those who are busy. These attitudes roll over into their schoolwork, too. Teachers tell me, "I can't motivate them because their parents don't require anything at home."

Defining Work

Many parents think that when children have sports practice and music lessons, that's enough. But these pursuits are disciplines of a different kind that have little to do with basic responsibility to the family.

Part of what goes on in the home is the development of teamwork. For family life to function, everyone depends on the contribution of everyone else. Household chores should be divided into two categories: routine contributions and extra jobs.

The routine—such as making beds, dusting furniture, and emptying the trash—should be part of the children's unpaid responsibilities. But the extras—those duties beyond their usual chores—should provide opportunities to earn additional money. The differences between the two divisions should be clearly defined within each family.

I grew up in a semi-tropical area of Australia where my father was head of an agricultural school. When the students were gone for the holidays, my two brothers, one sister, and I often pitched in to help Father care for the experimental research gardens. We always understood that some of the extra work would be rewarded. Children need to be in charge of a little bit of money, so I'm very much in favor of allowances. But it must be independent of their chores, unless the child is absolutely lazy and never makes any contribution. (Then curtailing the allowance would be a good motivator for most children.)

Hands-On Instruction

Nobody requires a mother to be "super*mom*." But one hat mothers should wear is that of super*visor*. We shouldn't expect to explain a job once, say "Do it" and have the task done. Even the best children don't work that way.

When you're with children, concentrate on hands-on instruction. Keep so close to your child that you can touch him. Children learn by conscious imitation and by unwitting imitation.

Instead of saying, "Go make your bed," do the task *with* the child. Get on one side of the bed and have your child on the other. Pull the sheet up and say, "Look, I've got wrinkles on my side," and make a sweeping movement with the hand, pushing out the creases. The child follows with the same smoothing motion.

Of course, a mom who works outside the home isn't going to do this as easily as a stay-at-home mom, but it can be done. The children of single mothers have to work with her because when she comes home her second job is waiting for her. I've seen single moms—and single dads—who are absolutely terrific in this area. They use the long stretches—especially the weekends—to catch up.

Let me encourage single parents here. One study show that many of the great scientists had only one parent.

Making Work Fun

When my children were little and were clearing the table and washing the dishes, I often made sure I had another job to do in the kitchen. As I put things away in the refrigerator, I told stories about my childhood—just as my father had done. They always loved the ones where I was slightly naughty.

We need to make chores as pleasant as possible. If you nag, the child will build up a negative attitude toward work. So when you're working with children, make it a happy time. Find things to laugh about. Don't always correct the child and make him feel helpless, especially in front of others.

My mother was a perfectionist. When my sisters and I did something wrong, she'd say, "There you go again. Just like Auntie Ida."

We dreaded that statement. Being compared to Aunt Ida was a character assassination because she hated doing anything and did that badly.

But when we worked with Father, he always built us up. He'd say, "My, you kids do a great job. You know, I didn't work like this when I was a kid. I'd sneak off and go hunting."

(We found out later from our grandmother he hadn't really been that naughty, but we loved his stories anyway.)

When the four of us were between the ages of six and 11, we loved working in the pea patch with Father. Thistles choked the plants, so it was up to us to keep the rows clean. We hoed the dirt and pulled the weeds, following Father's lead. When it was time to go back inside, believe me, we were hot and tired.

"Edith, come look at these kids!" he'd yell to Mother when we came home. "They worked all morning. I'm exhausted; I don't know how they kept up. They're great workers."

This prattle would go on for hours. My father really knew how to lay on encouragement. We received such a sense of accomplishment from our father that each of us is a keen gardener to this day.

And while we were leaning the principles of work, we also learned that there's a *best* way to do it.

If Father needed to correct us, he'd say, "Hmmm, let me see the way you're holding that hoe. You know, I've got a really tricky way to hold it. If you shift your hand this way, it's easier."

We watched Father lift his hoe just so, and we'd tilt it the same way.

I don't care how fumbling or poor their work is, children must never be robbed of the feeling that they can *do* it. And the parent, as supervisor, must always find something to praise, even if it's only to say, "I love your willing spirit."

It's Not Always Easy

Not all jobs are fun. This is where the need for consistency comes in. If one of the child's daily chores is to empty all the trash cans, the parent needs to see that he gets it done. Of course, children think up clever excuses. My favorite is when the child dramatically puts his hands to his head and moans, "I don't feel good, Mommy."

She must remain nonchalantly firm. Some children will drag their feet until finally the mom says, "Oh, forget it. I'll do it myself. It's sure quicker."

The minute a mother says that, she's lost the battle. Don't let that happen. Teaching children to do chores is part of your basic duty, even if it means slowing down and working with the child. Believe me, the extra effort pays off.

But don't expect precision from a child. Some children don't have the needed coordination to make a bed correctly. The parent must know what children are capable of at a certain age—and that will differ greatly.

If you have a nine-year-old who's capable of making his bed, don't let him ignore it. And keep "inspecting" his room, making sure he hasn't kicked anything under the bed or stuffed toys in drawers and wardrobes.

It is important to require the best that a child is capable of because the minute the child gets to school, the teachers require it. They aren't going to make much allowance for sloppiness. And when the child grows up and takes his first job, quality control is going to be very important. Sloppiness is a hard habit to break.

From a Young Age

How soon should your child start doing chores? That depends on his development. Children can be easily discouraged when they're assigned to do something they aren't capable of.

A good place to begin is with tidying up. Children can empty trash baskets and take care of their own possessions fairly early.

Even very young children can learn to take care of their toys. We have one grandchild in the family who was born orderly. Even at an early age, he put all his toys in rows in a small cabinet.

Second, every child can pick up clothes rather than tossing them in wild disarray. It also helps to have one particular spot for shoes and socks, so that the whole family isn't kept waiting Sunday morning. You can even teach young children to put their dirty clothes in the laundry basket.

Washing dishes can come later when the child has a fair amount of coordination. Most children like to set the table, but I wouldn't allow them to handle valuable china too early because we get angry if they break costly dishes. They can also fold up papers and arrange the magazines in the rack or on the coffee table.

Make sure your child *finishes* his chores. If he doesn't, call him back. He'll need to be called back in front of his friends only once.

When our children were little, I never let them go out to play until they'd checked with me. Otherwise, I discovered that if they thought after three jobs they could rush out to play, they did sloppy work. I always had the rule, "We are all going to work for the next hour and you can't go out to play whether you finish your job or not." Then they had no incentive to rush it.

Occasionally, a child will say he's finished his work early, so I check it then.

Of course, this constant supervision is hard work on you. But you'll find that *your* hard work will pay off in the life of your child. And isn't that worth it?

Jean Lush, a family counselor in Seattle, continues the family work traditions with her nine grandchildren.

8

Making Bible Memorization Fun

Betty B. Robertson

*M*y husband, Earl, and I are convinced children should experience joy and satisfaction from hiding God's Word in their hearts. But when we suggested rote memorization to our son and daughter, who were then nine and six, they merely stared at us.

If we wanted them to think positively about the Bible, we'd have to make memorization *fun*.

In the days following, we asked the Lord for special ideas, read curriculum books, and searched our own memories for childhood activities we had enjoyed. Gradually, we came up with several ideas that turned our children's attitudes around. Perhaps some will help add spark to your family, too.

The first step is to choose verses you believe are important for your children to memorize, keeping in mind the developmental level of each child. Some denominations offer Bible memorization programs that are helpful.

Children learn faster if they understand what they're memorizing. Be prepared to explain any words your children don't know and to clarify the meaning of the verse or passage.

Then choose a technique:

Balloon Pop

Let your child help blow up balloons. Then with a marker, write one word of the verse on each balloon. Tape them to the wall and read the verse together. The children take turns popping any balloon with a pin, followed by everyone saying the verse together. Another balloon is popped, and the entire verse repeated. Continue until all the balloons have been burst.

Chalkboard Fun

After the children print the verse on the board, they take turns erasing a word. Each time a word is erased, everyone says the verse, supplying the missing words. Continue until all words have been deleted.

Hide and Seek

Have your children cut out different shapes of construction paper on which you write one word from the verse. Say the verse together. Then have the children leave the room while you hide the shapes. When the children return, they look for the shapes, put them together in the correct order and say the verse. Continue playing for as long as interest remains high.

Hopscotch

If the weather is nice, draw the traditional pattern on your driveway or front walk. In bad weather, you can use masking tape to make the pattern on the floor of your largest room. Write each word of the verse on separate cards and tape them into each hopscotch box. As the children hop through the grid, they recite the verse as they go.

Individual Envelope Puzzles

Put each word of a verse on a paper strip and tuck them into separate envelopes—one for each child. Write the reference on the outside of the envelopes so the child can look up the verse and put the words together in the right order.

Jigsaw Puzzle

Have each child print a verse on a piece of posterboard and decorate it with a border. Then each draws puzzle lines and cuts out the pieces. As they put the puzzle together, they say the verse.

Line Up the Cans

On three-by-five cards, write one word from the chosen verse and include the reference. Tape the cards to cans from your pantry and stack them randomly on the table. Have each child take turns putting them in the right order. Say the verse together. Take away one can at a time and quote the entire verse after each removal.

Memory Verse Tree

Select a suitable tree branch from your yard. Spray-paint it, if desired, and prop it up in a bucket of sand for a year-round Scripture tree. Then in each season, have your children make appropriate "leaves" out of construction paper: February, hearts; December, Christmas trees or ornaments; March, shamrocks; and October, red maples or yellow aspens.

Print the Scripture verse on one side of the leaf, the reference on the other. Place the leaves in a box near the memory verse tree.

One child chooses a leaf and reads the Scripture reference to another family member, who then tries to say the verse. If it is said correctly, the leaf is place on the tree.

Nerf Ball Throw

All family members look up a designated verse and memorize it, so they will be prepared to play. Choose one child to be "it" and give him the ball. He says the verse and then throws the ball to someone else, who says the verse again. Continue until everyone has said the verse several times. You might also choose to say only one word of a verse each time the ball is caught, until the entire Scripture has been quoted.

Promise Box

Provide three-by-five index cards on which your children can write the verses you've selected. Give each child a suitable-sized box and let him decorate it. The Scripture cards may be kept in the promise box and studied.

Tape or Video Recording

Let the children take turns quoting verses into the microphone of a cassette player or in front of a video camera. Play the tape back. They'll enjoy hearing their own voices or seeing themselves on TV.

Verse Box

Cut large holes—about three inches apart—in an empty cereal box. Have the children cut out shapes from construction paper on which you write the reference and a word from the verse. Tape a long piece of yarn to the back of each shape and have the children drop these into the box in the right order, saying the verse in unison.

Then take turns pulling a word from the box, quoting the Scripture each time. Continue until all the shapes are removed and the verse is said from memory.

Vowel Hunt

Classified ads from your local newspaper make a good background on which to print. Use a felt tip marker and write the Bible verse, leaving out all the vowels, The children supply the vowels to fill each space and then take turns repeating the Scripture.

Word Hunt

Print the verse on a sheet of classified ads, omitting some of the words. Print the omitted words on suitable-sized pieces of paper and place them in a box. The children take turns hunting through the box to find the missing words and placing them in the blank spots.

These are just some of the ideas that have worked for us. As you ask the Lord to help you present His Word in creative ways, He will help you come up with even more.

Betty B. Robertson estimates her two children have memorized over 200 verses over the years. She and her family live in Roanoke, Virginia.

☙ 9

Send Your Children to Another World This Summer

Ray Seldomridge

*P*ulcifer had a problem. Despite the efforts of his parents, teachers and the local librarian, he simply could not stop reading books, so he never had time for TV.

"When I was your age, you couldn't pry me away from the television set," said Pulcifer's disappointed father. "I'd always hoped that my own son would follow in my footsteps."

What finally happened to Pulcifer? You'll have to read *The*

Problem with Pulcifer by Florence Parry Heide to find out. (Groan.)
This is a trick to send you off to the public library, where you can find
out about reading programs for your children. Unless Pulcifer is your
child, you many need to offer a little encouragement to your young
readers. You still have time to show your kids that reading can be fun.

More parents and children than ever before are turning to reading
as a pastime. Not long ago, 750 boys and girls in a Los Angeles
suburb read 12,000 books over an eight-week period. Enrollment in
the library's reading club had doubled in just three years, and a lec-
ture by Jim Trelease (author of *The Read-Aloud Handbook*) drew a
packed auditorium of interested parents.

So don't believe it when you hear someone say this is the age of
video, and all kids do nowadays is sit in front of the TV. Children's
books are rolling off the presses in record numbers, and parents are
snatching up armloads of them faster than compact disks.

Few of these parents have ever read an essay or article on why
books are important—ponderous prose from an educator saying
things like "books teach children basic moral values" or "reading will
broaden your child's perspective and give him a zest for life." Those
statements are as boring as they are true. Instead, parents understand
the value of reading because they themselves are readers.

"It doesn't take an educational study," writes Betsy Hearne in
Choosing Books for Children," to show that children do what you do,
not what you tell them to do. If you like to read to yourself and your
children, they will like reading to themselves and their children."

On a similar note, Jim Trelease tells his predominantly female
audiences that if Dad always picks up a ball instead of a book, his
children may be getting the message that athletics are more important than reading. Suppose that you are a bookworm, and the local
library has a summer program that promises glittering prizes to kids
who will read. What if your son or daughter still hasn't heard the
siren call? Well, there's a number of ways you might successfully
beckon a child into this world of unimaginable delights. Here are a
few ideas:

Capitalize on you child's other interests. If your eight-year-old son wants to do nothing but play computer games, show him a book or two on computer programming. Maybe he'll create his own games, and learn a lot while doing it. Or if your 12-year-old daughter spends most of her time trying on clothes, a book like *Just Victoria* (David C. Cook) will catch her interest as she relates to another girl who's becoming boy-conscious.

Offer to extend bedtime for the purpose of reading. During the summer months, it won't hurt to have even a five-year-old go to sleep a half-hour later than usual. But the child has to be in his or her bed, quietly reading or looking at the pictures during that time. If your son or daughter takes you up on this offer, be ready to provide a bedside lamp and lots of good print material.

Reward book reading with more books! Tell your kids that for every five (or two, or 10) books they read, you'll let them pick out a new one for purchase at the bookstore. Unless you're terribly rich, you may need to limit their selection to quality paperbacks. But children who have a chance to build their own libraries are more likely to become lifetime page-turners.

Read aloud as a family. Whether your children are infants or high-schoolers, reading aloud together is indispensable. And everyone is doing it! Professors at Oxford University read literature to their students, just as Ezra the scribe got the nation of Israel off to a fresh start by reading aloud the law of Moses for six hours straight (Nehemiah 8:1-3).

Try to read aloud every night. You will find it an easy habit to stick to, as long as you select books that appeal to you as much as they do to your kids.

Leave books lying around the house. What do you suppose would happen if you put boxes of chocolates by the telephone, in the bathroom, and on the kitchen table? Presto, they'd get eaten. Likewise, colorful, interesting books left in these places will get read. Try it, and don't forget to change the books (from the library, of course) every week. Also be sure your home has at least one good reading area and a book rack full of assorted temptations.

Build reading into your family traditions. Already many families celebrate Christmas Day by reading the Nativity story in Luke 2, and even Dicken's *Christmas Carol*. But family life is full of other settings that need a good book for a crowning jewel. Try sharing *Charlotte's Web* together at the time of the county fair, or *Mr. Revere and I* on July 4th.

All these ideas are worth your attention if you want books to play an important role in your children's development. But two bits of advice should also be mentioned:

• You will probably have to limit TV viewing hours. Children who eat junk food aren't as likely to touch their dinners, or to read books . . . , if they've been lulled into passivity by Pandora's electric box.

• Don't hurry your children into reading. If encouraged by read-aloud parents and enticed by available books, they will read when they are good and ready. To keep your children motivated, here are some pointers.

Let each library trip become an adventure. Wander the aisles together and familiarize yourselves with the types of books available. Are you looking for picture books for the very young, beginning readers for your six-to eight-year-old, or short novels for the later elementary grades? Does your son or daughter want suspenseful mysteries, sports stories, hobby books, fantasies, classics, biographies, historical fiction, poetry, animal tales, folklore, factual science books, or a mixture of these?

Let your children decide. You can help guide them in their reading tastes, but ultimately only *they* know what they want. Encourage a variety of reading so that they learn what's available.

Trust your judgment. "Taste" a page or two. If a book seems to be lacking, put it down and try another. Dabble a lot.

Go for whatever is good and uplifting. Naturally, your first impulse will be to look for books from Christian publishers. If so, search for those that are well-written and have interesting, believable characters (rather than being "preachy").

Try such tales as *The Tanglewoods' Secret* by Patricia M. St. John or *A Horse Named Cinnamon* by Jeanne Bovde. Also, don't forget the many creative Bible story books, including Tomie de Paola's *Queen Esther* for younger children.

Much so-called "secular" literature also abounds with Christian moral values and theological truths. Don't miss this treasure trove, which includes *Little House on the Prairie, Robinson Crusoe, Anne of Green Gables* and dozens of other gems.

Moreover, don't fear such fantastic tales as C. S. Lewis' *Chronicles of Narnia* or Robert Siegel's *Alpha Centauri.* As you may know, much of today's fantasy literature is abhorrent because it dwells upon evil and glorifies ungodliness. But Christian fantasy parallels Scripture itself in the effective and proper use of good versus evil imagery. Such stories help young readers grasp at a deeply emotional level the fact that evil cannot ultimately triumph. (Some well-meaning Christian parents avoid anything to do with fire-breathing dragons, forgetting that this symbol for evil is used in the Bible itself—in Revelation 12:7. What matters is that the dragon is defeated!)

Get recommendations. Ask your friends about the books they've read. Scan the library's recommended reading lists. You may even want to obtain a copy of *Books Children Love* by Elizabeth Wilson (Crossway), a fine annotated bibliography written especially for Christian parents.

Okay, okay. Here's what happened to Pulcifer. He was sent to a special corrective remedial class for non-TV watchers, and then to a psychiatrist. Neither ploy worked.

"We've done all we can," said his mother. "No one can say we haven't tried."

Assured by his father that they loved him anyway, Pulcifer "settled down comfortably with his new stack of library books."

End of story. But not a bad beginning for you and your children this summer.

Ray Seldomridge is editorial director of the youth periodicals published by Focus on the Family.

10

Hot Ideas for Summertime

Elaine Hardt

After school's been out for several weeks, the novelty of summer quickly wears off. Meanwhile, when the temperature heads toward three digits, a family's impatience can rise, too.

You don't have to mark time until the school bell rings again. Here are 11 ways to to have a memorable summer of fun *and* learning:

Show That Housecleaning Can Be Fun

Well, that might be a slight exaggeration. But don't call it "housework"—refer instead to "The Challenge of the Day." Have the kids predict how long it will take to clean a room and then set the timer. Put a peppy tape on the stereo and tackle the cleaning together.

When my sons helped, we listened to lively Greek folk music as we dusted and picked up. I also found that the task was completed best if I worked *with* them. Children are often overwhelmed when we send them into a room and say, "Clean it." It's far more effective to ask, "What do we need to do in here today?"

It helps to be a little zany, too. I often escorted my sons into their room and announced, "Let's get going here. I'll start with the sheets." Then I'd toss several coins under their beds, so once they started hauling toys and T-shirts out into the open, they'd discover an immediate reason for continuing. Even on the days when I didn't toss coins, they cleaned under the bed—just in case I had hidden a nickel under a loose sock.

Encouragement Works Wonders

Of course you can do the housework better—and faster—than the kids, but efficiency is not the name of the game. Helping your children learn responsibility is your goal.

Explain why a certain job is important, and then demonstrate how you want it completed. Have the child try it while you're watching. Encourage a lot. My mother always said I was her "good little helper." That simple expression of appreciation made me work all the harder. What a great attitude when you compare it to that of a visiting aunt who berated me for missing a spot on the table when I dusted.

Since I tried to keep tension out of my cleaning sessions, my sons would occasionally ask if their next-door buddy, Danny, could help. Then they'd go to his house and work with *his* chores so they could all play outside.

It's okay to remind children that someday they'll need to know how to houseclean. Even 10-year-old boys are thinking, *When I have my own place, I can have my own things on the shelf and my own food in the refrigerator.* So as we'd clean, I'd say such things as "I know this looks like something Mom should do, but you'll need to know this someday." Today, Peter helps his wife around the house, and Robert is an unmarried fire fighter and paramedic. Both have put that early training to good use.

Produce Your Own Dramas

Help your children dig out old clothes and design costumes for a play about your family. Mom and Dad, this is for you, too—makeup and all. Check the local thrift shops for unusual outfits to use in acting out a favorite Bible story. Use scrap material to turn a child into a tree or animal. You might ask family and neighbors to join your impromptu productions as well. Don't forget to take pictures for the album.

When our sons were little, there weren't many kids in the neighborhood, so we didn't put on pageants often. But the boys still had fun. One of their favorite dramas was simply called "Sunday School." They lined their stuffed animals up on the sofa to listen to then seven-year-old Peter "preach." His younger brother, Robert, was the usher and would pass the basket to the animals. The offerings were pretty slim until they came up with the idea to supply all of their "parishioners" with Monopoly money.

Introduce Your Pre-Teens to the Kitchen

When you turn the kids loose with your cookbook collection, some interesting ideas can evolve, especially as you let them create their own "restaurant" with place mats, centerpieces, and assorted props.

Our boys liked to ham it up. When it was their day to cook, they drew pencil mustaches on their faces and spoke in false French accents. Other days, they turned our kitchen table into "Pete's Cafe" or "Rob's Diner." As preparation for their taking over the kitchen, I had gradually given them practice in browning the meat or peeling the potatoes. I also taught them how to clean up.

Round Up Odds and Ends

Do you have any old appliances or electronic equipment (toasters, mixers, tape players, or VCRs) gathering dust in the garage? If you do, let your youngsters take them apart (under your supervision, of course) and see what they're all about.

While you're at it, look at what's lying around the house with an eye for science. You can do a lot with magnets or a magnifying glass, sand, dirt, and pebbles. And don't think that sandboxes are only for toddlers. My husband, Don, expanded our boys' sandbox when they were in elementary school, and they spent hours constructing cities and roads—with only sand, water, and twigs.

Make Bug Corrals

Staking out a square foot of the backyard with popsicle sticks and observing bugs gives an interesting view into a child's world. Our desert area provided numerous creatures to look at. I hadn't been interested in bugs, but when our sons were toddlers, they were so close to the ground that they saw them anyway and had me looking at them, too.

Soon, I discovered that it's fun to make "stick corrals" and watch what's coming and going. As the boys got older and began to ask questions about the specific kinds of insects we were watching, I would say, "Let's see if we can find that in one of our books." Their curiosity eventually led to their own research.

Explore the Library

On hot afternoons, the local library provides a great place for the whole family. I always liked taking a packet of file cards to jot down a couple of sentences about any books the boys might be interested in later. I'd note the author and title and then file the cards alphabetically so we could refer to them later.

Churches can really help families here, since public libraries don't have many Christian books. Biographies are especially good because they provide plots for homemade dramas and examples in dealing with challenges such as discouragement and temptation.

Read Together

If your youngster isn't ready for independent reading, you can read a page for him, using your most entertaining and dramatic voice.

Then let your child read the next page. Encourage the young reader to have fun and even "ham it up." Fill in the mispronounced words without comment. Stop in the middle of the story and talk about how the book began, the setting, and the characters. Ask your children what they think might happen by the end. Then read on and see how the story concludes.

For our family, this was always a bedtime ritual, so we'd sit in our robes and jammies and read together. The time was too special to be rushed. The boys especially enjoyed pondering such questions as "Is this what Dad would say?" or "What would Moses have done?"

Use the Tape Recorder

Most kids will enjoy reading a story into the tape recorder. Our boys loved to make sound effects, too, such as beating their chests with cupped hands to make the sound of galloping horses. Other times they'd devise ways to make the sound of thunder or rain.

Today, children who have grown up with television are often fascinated by the sound effects of radio dramas. Even showing them how glasses filled with different levels of water produce different sounds will be interesting to them.

Display Bible Verses

Let the children make verse posters. A hallway can become an art gallery of beautifully illustrated Scripture.

We had a short hallway, so our refrigerator held most of the boys' art. Don and I don't have anyone decorating our hall now, so we print verses in large print on our computer and send them to our grandchildren to color for the hospital patients their parents visit. We also print the verses for the Sunday school children in our church to color for our hospital visits. When we ask patients if they would like to keep them, no one has refused. They are blessed by having the Word of God around them.

Find Ways to Serve Others

Have a family meeting to choose a Christian service project you can do for the summer. Maybe you'll opt for a weekly visit to an elderly person in your neighborhood or find ways to spruce up the church yard.

Our boys pulled weeds at church, wrote letters to out-of-town relatives, and visited an elderly neighbor and her plump little dog. In the heat of our summers, our bushes don't bloom, but we'd occasionally gather a bouquet of interesting desert weeds for those visits.

By now, you may be thinking, *All this takes time. I'm already too busy.* Of course, making the most of summer takes a little planning, cooperation, and enthusiasm. But you'll be amazed at the creativity that blossoms under your guidance. It may help to remember there will never be another summer quite like this one. Your kids will never be the same again. And many of these "teachable moments" will be lost forever.

Our sons are too quickly grown now and living away from home. As I watch our grandchildren's eyes widen when their dad pours red-colored water into blue-colored water to make purple-colored water, it's like peeping into the past at the activities I used to enjoy with Peter and Robert.

As adults help children discover their world, they are also reminding the little ones that they are appreciated and are truly a blessing. Isn't that worth the effort?

Elaine Hardt teaches third grade in Phoenix, Arizona.

PART THREE

FOCUS ON
TEENAGERS

11

Surviving Your Child's Stormy Teen Years

James C. Dobson, Ph.D.

*I*n my second film series entitled, "Turn Your Heart Toward Home," I offered this advice to parents of teenagers: "Get 'em through it." That may not sound like such a stunning idea, but I believe it has merit for most families—especially those with one or more tough-minded kids.

When parents of strong-willed children look ahead to the adolescent river, they often expect an early encounter with rapids to give way to swirling currents and life-threatening turbulence. If that doesn't turn over their teenagers' boats, they seem destined to drown farther downstream when they plunge over the falls.

Fortunately, the typical journey is much safer than anticipated. The river usually descends not into the falls, but into smooth water once more. Even though your teenager may be splashing and thrashing and gasping for air, it is not likely that his boat will capsize. It is more buoyant than you might think.

Yes, a few individuals do go over the falls, usually because of drug abuse. Even some of them climb back into the canoe and paddle on down the river. In fact, the greatest danger of sinking the boat could come from . . . *you!*

This warning is addressed particularly to idealistic and perfectionistic parents who are determined to make their adolescents—*all* of them—perform and achieve and measure up to the highest standard. A perfectionist, by the way, is a person who takes great pains with what he does and then gives them to everyone else. In so doing, he rocks a boat that is already threatened by the rapids.

Perhaps another child could handle the additional turbulence, but our concern is for the unsteady kid—the one who lacks common sense for a while and may even lean toward irrational behavior. Don't unsettle his boat any more than you must!

Majors and Minors

I'm reminded of a waitress who recognized me when I came into the restaurant where she worked. She was not busy that day and wanted to talk about her 12-year-old daughter. As a single mother, she had gone through severe struggles with the girl, whom she identified as being *very* strong-willed.

"We have fought tooth and nail for this entire year," she said. "It has been awful! We argue nearly every night, and most of our fights are over the same issue."

I asked her what had caused the conflict, and she replied, "My daughter is still a little girl, but she wants to shave her legs. I feel she's too young to be doing that, and she becomes so angry that she won't even talk to me. This has been the worst year of our lives together."

I looked at the waitress and exclaimed, "Lady, buy your daughter a razor!"

That 12-year-old girl was paddling into a time of life that would rock her canoe good and hard. As a single parent, Mom would soon be trying to keep this rebellious kid from getting into drugs, alcohol, sex and pregnancy, early marriage, school failure, and the possibility of running away. Truly, there would be many ravenous alligators in her river within a year or two. In that setting, it seemed unwise to make a big deal over what was essentially a non-issue.

While I agreed with the mother that adolescence should not be rushed into prematurely, there were higher goals than maintaining a proper developmental timetable.

I have seen other parents fight similar battles over nonessentials, such as the purchase of a first bra for a flat-chested pre-adolescent girl.

For goodness sake! If she wants it that badly, she probably needs if for social reasons. Run, don't walk, to the nearest department store and buy her a bra.

The objective, as Charles and Andy Stanley wrote, is to *keep your kids on your team.* Don't throw away your friendship over behavior that has no great moral significance. There will be plenty of real issues that require you to stand like a rock. Save your big guns for those crucial confrontations.

Let me make it very clear, again, that this advice is not relevant to every teenager. The compliant kid who is doing wonderfully in school, has great friends, is disciplined in his conduct, and loves his parents is not nearly so delicate. Perhaps his parents can urge him to reach even higher standards in his achievements and lifestyle.

My concern, however, is for that youngster who *could* go over the falls. He is intensely angry at home and is being influenced by a carload of crummy friends. Be very careful with him. Pick and choose what is worth fighting for, and settle for something less than perfection on issues that don't really matter. *Just get him through it!*

What does this mean in practical terms? It may indicate a willingness to let his room look like a junkyard for a while. Does that surprise you? I don't like lazy, sloppy, undisciplined kids any more than you do, but given the possibilities for chaos that this angry boy or girl might precipitate, spit-shined rooms may not be all that important.

The philosophy we applied with our teenagers (and you might try with yours) can be called "loosen and tighten." By this I mean we tried to loosen our grip on everything that had no lasting significance and tighten down on everything that did. We said "yes" whenever we possibly could, to give support to the occasional "no." And most importantly, we tried never to get too far away from our kids emotionally.

It is simply not prudent to write off a son or daughter, no matter how foolish, irritating, selfish, or insane a child may seem to be. You need to be there not only while their canoe is bouncing precariously, but after the river runs smoothly again.

You have the remainder of your life to reconstruct the relationship that is now in jeopardy. Don't let anger fester for too long. Make the first move toward reconciliation. And try hard not to hassle your kids. They *hate* to be nagged. If you follow them around with one complaint after another, they are almost forced to protect themselves by appearing deaf.

And finally, continue to treat them with respect, even when punishment or restrictions are necessary. Occasionally, you may even need to say, "I'm sorry!"

My father found it very difficult to say those words. I remember working with him in the backyard when I was 15 years of age, on a day when he was particularly irritable for some reason. I probably deserved his indignation, but I thought he was being unfair. He crabbed at me for everything I did, even when I hustled. Finally, he yelled at me for something petty and that did it. He capsized my canoe. I threw down the rake and quit. Defiantly I walked across our property and down the street while my dad demanded that I come back.

It was one of the few times I ever took him on like that! I mean-dered around town for awhile, wondering what would happen to me when I finally went home. Then I strolled over to my cousin's house on the other side of town. After several hours there, I admitted to his father that I had had a bad fight with my dad and he didn't know where I was. My uncle persuaded me to call home and assure my parents that I was safe. With knees quaking, I phoned my dad.

"Stay there," he said, "I'm coming over."

To say that I was apprehensive for the next few minutes would be an understatement. In a short time Dad arrived and asked to see me alone.

"Bo," he began. "I didn't treat you right this afternoon. I was riding your back for no good reason, and I want you to know I'm sorry. You mom and I want you to come on home now."

He made a friend for life.

Maintain a Reserve Army

A good military general will never commit all his troops to combat at the same time. He maintains a reserve force that can relieve the exhausted soldiers when they falter on the front lines. I wish parents of adolescents would implement the same strategy. Instead, they commit every ounce of their energy and every second of their time to the business of living, holding nothing in reserve for the challenge of the century. It is a classic mistake which can be dis-astrous for parents of strong-willed adolescents. Let me explain.

The problem begins with a basic misunderstanding during the pre-school years. I hear mothers say, "I don't plan to work until the kids are in kindergarten. Then I'll get a job."

They appear to believe that the heavy demands on them will end magically when they get their youngest in school. In reality, the teen years will generate as much pressure on them as did the preschool era. An adolescent turns a house upside down . . . literally and figu-ratively. Not only is the typical rebellion of those years an extremely stressful experience, but the chauffeuring, supervising, cooking, and cleaning required to support an adolescent can be exhausting.

Someone within the family must reserve the energy to cope with those new challenges. Mom is the candidate of choice. Remember, too, that menopause and a man's mid-life crisis are scheduled to coincide with adolescence, which makes a wicked soup! It is a wise mother who doesn't exhaust herself at a time when so much is going on at home.

I know it is easier to talk about maintaining a lighter schedule than it is to secure one. It is also impractical to recommend that mothers not seek formal employment during this era. Millions of women have to work for economic reasons, including the rising number of single parents in our world. Others choose to pursue busy careers. That is a decision to be made by a woman and her husband, and I would not presume to tell them what to do.

But decisions have inevitable consequences. In this case, there are biophysical forces at work which simply must be reckoned with. If, for example, 80 percent of a woman's available energy in a given day is expended in getting dressed, driving to work, doing her job for eight or 10 hours, and stopping by the grocery store on the way home—then there is only 20 percent left for everything else.

Maintenance of the family, cooking meals, cleaning the kitchen, relating to her husband, and all other personal activities must be powered by that diminishing resource. It is no wonder that her batteries are spent by the end of the day. Weekends should be restful, but they are usually not. Thus, she plods through the years on her way to burnout.

This is my point: A woman in this situation has thrown all her troops into front-line combat. She is already exhausted, but there is no reserve on which to call. In that weakened condition, the routine stresses of raising an adolescent can be overwhelming.

Let me say it again. Raising boisterous teenagers is an exciting and rewarding but also a frustrating experience. Their radical highs and lows affect our moods. The noise, the messes, the complaints, the arguments, the sibling rivalry, the missed curfews, the paced floors, the wrecked car, the failed test, the jilted lover, the wrong friends, the busy telephone, the pizza on the carpet, the ripped new blouse, the rebellion, the slammed doors, the mean words, the tears—it's enough to drive a *rested* mother crazy.

But what about our career woman who already "gave at the office," then came home to this chaos? Any unexpected crisis or even a minor irritant can set off a torrent of emotion. There is no reserve on which to draw. In short, the parents of adolescents should save some energy with which to cope with aggravation.

Whether or not you are able to accept and implement my advice is your business. It is mine to offer, and this is my best shot: To help you get through the turbulence of adolescence, you should:

- *Keep the schedule simple.*
- *Get plenty of rest.*
- *Eat nutritious meals.*
- *Stay on your knees.*

When fatigue leads adults to act like hot-tempered teenagers, anything can happen at home.

The Desperate Need for Fathers

It is stating the obvious, I suppose, to say that fathers of rebellious teenagers are desperately needed at home during those years. In their absence, mothers are left to handle disciplinary problems alone. This is occurring in millions of families headed by single mothers today, and I know how tough their task has become.

Not only are they doing a job that should have been shouldered by two; they must also deal with behavioral problems that fathers are more ideally suited to handle. It is generally understood that a man's larger size, deeper voice, and masculine demeanor make it easier for him to deal with defiance in the younger generation.

Likewise, I believe the exercise of authority is a mantle ascribed to him by the Creator. Not only are fathers needed to provide leadership and discipline during the adolescent years, but they can be highly influential on their sons during this period of instability.

Someone has said, "Link a boy to the right man and he seldom goes wrong." I believe that is true. If a dad and his son can develop hobbies together or other common interests, the rebellious years can pass in relative tranquillity. What they experience may be remembered for a lifetime. Let me address the reader directly: What common ground are you cultivating with your impressionable son? Some fathers build or repair cars with them; some construct small models or make things in a woodshop.

My dad and I hunted and fished together. There is no way to describe what those days meant to me as we entered the woods in the early hours of the morning. How could I get angry at this man who took time to be with me? We had wonderful talks while coming home from a day of laughter and fun in the country.

I've tried to maintain that kind of contact with my son, Ryan. We rebuilt a Model A Ford together. We also hunted rabbits, quail, pheasant, and larger game since he turned 12. As it was with my father, Ryan and I have had some meaningful conversations while out in the fields together.

One year, for example, we got up one morning and situated ourselves in a deer blind before the break of day. About 20 yards away from us was a feeder which operated on a timer. At 7 A.M., it automatically dropped kernels of corn into a pan below.

Ryan and I huddled together in this blind, talking softly about whatever came to mind. Then through the fog, we saw a beautiful doe emerge silently into the clearing. She took several minutes to get to the feeder near where we were hiding. We had no intention of shooting her, but it was fun to watch this beautiful animal from close range. She was extremely wary, sniffing the air and listening for the sounds of danger.

Finally, she inched her way to the feeder, still looking around skittishly as though sensing our presence. Then she ate a quick breakfast and fled.

I whispered to Ryan, "There is something valuable to be learned from what we have just seen. Whenever you come upon a free supply of high-quality corn, unexpectedly provided right there in the middle of the forest, be careful! The people who put it there are probably sitting nearby in a blind just waiting to take a shot at you. Keep your eyes and ears open!"

Ryan may not always remember that advice, but *I* will. It isn't often a father says something that he considers profound to his teenage son. One thing is certain: This interchange and the other ideas we shared on that day would not have occurred at home. Opportunities for that kind of communication have to be created. And it's worth working to achieve.

This chapter is adapted from *Parenting Isn't for Cowards*, by James C. Dobson, Ph.D. Copyright © 1987 Word Publishing, Dallas, Texas. All rights reserved.

12

Helping Your Teen Say No to Sex

Josh McDowell

Dear Mr. McDowell,
    Having premarital sex was the most horrifying experience of my life. It wasn't at all the emotionally satisfying experience the world deceived me into believing. I felt as if my insides were being exposed and my heart left unattended. I know God has forgiven me of this haunting sin, but I also know I can never have my virginity back. I dread the day that I have to tell the man I truly love and wish to marry that he is not the only one—though I wish he were. I have stained my life—a stain that will never come out.

Monica

I would be encouraged if Monica's situation were the exception to the rule and that most of our youth from Christian homes were not struggling with premarital sex, but it's not.

Consider our "Why Wait?" study in the late 1980s on teen sexual attitudes and behavior in the evangelical church. We scientifically surveyed 1,400 kids and learned that by age 18, 43 percent of churched youth have engaged in sexual intercourse, and another 18 percent have fondled breasts or genitals. Additionally, 36 percent of the youths said they were *not* able to state that sexual intercourse was morally unacceptable before marriage!

My wife, Dottie, and I are the proud parents of four children. We don't want them to suffer the pain that Monica and thousands of others have experienced. Yet, unless we take definitive steps to reverse the trends, the moral convictions of our children may also be eroded.

At every turn society tells our kids: "If it feels good, do it" and "Life only comes around once, live it to the fullest now!" The radio screeches out songs like "Tonight's the Night" and MTV vividly illustrates lewd and suggestive lyrics. By and large, secular broadcast media do little to reinforce moral values or demonstrate the consequences of irresponsible moral behavior. When was the last time you saw a secular TV program show a person contracting a sexually transmitted disease or portray a broken teenager suffering through an unplanned pregnancy?

Society's false and distorted messages on love and sex are having a devastating affect on the basic moral convictions of our young people. Those basic moral convictions once held by a previous generation are apparently not being passed on to our present generation. And a generation without moral convictions is a generation crumbling under the pressures of a secular world view.

History shows that when a generation fails to know *why* they believe what they believe, their convictions are in danger of being undermined. Today, perhaps more than at any other time, we lack a "sexual apologetic"—a sound defense for our moral convictions. As one 18-year-old told me: "I was asking questions about Christianity and not having them answered. I was seeking reasons not to have premarital sex and couldn't find any." If your child and mine don't learn why God said to wait until marriage to enjoy sex, they will lack the foundational basis for their moral convictions.

The Bible is quite clear on this subject. For when Paul admonished, ". . . this is the will of God, your sanctification; that is that you abstain from sexual immorality" (1 Thes. 4:3), he did so in the positive. One of the greatest truths you can share with your child about saying no is that inherent within every negative command in the Bible there are two positive principles: 1) it is meant to protect us, and 2) to provide for us.

God knows that if sex is going to be meaningful, it must be experienced within a loving commitment of marriage. His laws, restrictions, and commands are actually for our good (Deut. 10:12-13). They establish the boundaries and guidelines that define maximum love, relationships, and sex.

As much as possible, explain to your children this basic truth behind the restrictions God places upon them. Be sure to communicate that both you and God want only what is best for them. Eventually the point will get through; you love them and your loving limits—that come from a loving God—are to protect and provide for them.

Here are effective arguments—from spiritual, emotional, and physical perspectives—that you can use to describe the reason why God wants your child to wait until marriage to enjoy sexual relations.

Protection from God's Judgment

Fundamentally, there is only one primary reason to abstain from premarital sex—because God says so. There are many reasons He gives for prohibiting us, but His "Thou shalt not's" should be sufficient when we believe His restrictions are for our best interests. Hebrews 13:4 says that "marriage should be honored by all, and the marriage bed kept pure, for God will judge the adulterer and all the sexually immoral."

When the Bible says we reap what we sow, it would certainly

apply to immoral acts. Judgment will surely fall on the disobedient—a good reason to follow the commands that God has given to us.

Protect the Mind from Sexual Comparisons

Some of the most beautiful relationships I have seen were destroyed through the programming of the most important and sensitive sex organ—the mind. One of the fallouts of premarital sex is the continual fear of sexual comparison—comparing the sexual performance of one against the other. A mind programmed with unhealthy sexual experiences can come back to haunt us as "sexual ghosts."

Scores of young people have told how they battle with the fear of sexual comparison. In many cases, it has actually been the cause of breaking up relationships. Give an example to your child from your own life or the life of another of how "reruns in the theater of the mind" cause problems before and after marriage.

Protect from Suspicion and Provide Trust

Most marriage counselors will tell you that one of the key factors to a fulfilled marriage and sexual relationship is *trust*. And premarital sex, to varying degrees, erodes the trust factor in a relationship.

When a husband or wife knows the other has waited to have sex until after marriage, it strengthens that trust factor. And one of the best motivations for continued fidelity in marriage is again *trust*. If you waited in your own relationship, share with your child how waiting secured trust in your marriage.

Share all these truths convincingly within the positive context of God's provision and protection. But while the reasons to wait are important to helping your child say no to sexual pressures, they only address one side of the problem. The flip side involves a close relationship between you and your child.

Protect from Fear and Provide Peace of Mind

Today, perhaps more than any other time, there is widespread fear of contracting a sexually transmitted disease. In the next 24 hours, more than 35,000 Americans will get a sexually transmitted disease—that's 13 million people in the next year! A few years ago, there were just five of these diseases—today there are more than 34. And with the advent of the killer AIDS virus, medical doctors are becoming prophets of doom.

Surgeon General C. Everett Koop and others predict that unless cures are found or lifestyles are changed by the year 2000, our plague-stricken generation could be sterile or give birth to more infected or deformed children.

God wants to protect us from the nightmare of being infected with diseases and provide us with peace of mind. God certainly had our children's best interest at heart when He said that we should abstain from sexual immorality (1 Thes. 4:3).

Rules Without a Relationship Equal Rebellion

Danny was from a Christian home and had come to me for advice. "Sometimes I feel so alone—like no one cares," he said. "My folks live in their adult world, and I live in my teenage world. It didn't always seem to be that way. I know it sounds crazy, but I want them to leave me alone and yet, I want to be a part of their lives."

Danny looked up and gazed past me as he spoke more slowly. "Most of the time, they do leave me alone and it gets pretty lonely."

I'm afraid Danny's feelings, representative of so many today, are a contributing cause of sexual involvement. Studies show that of those teens that are sexually active, 58 percent feel they have never gotten to know their fathers and 40 percent believe they have never gotten to know their mothers.

This sense of feeling alienated from the family is one reason why many young people are extremely susceptible to sexual involvement. Yet, it is not sex they are seeking. A young lady wrote me recently and in three succinct sentences identified where millions of young people are at today:

Mr. McDowell,
 I wish someone would just love me (but not physically). I want

someone to show me they care. I want to be loved, but I don't know how to accept it or give it.

If I were asked to list the contributing factors to our teenage sexual crisis, at the top of my list would be adolescent alienation brought on partly by parental inattentiveness. If you want to reduce the sexual pressures your child will undoubtedly face, develop a close relationship of mutual love and respect. Establishing sexual prohibitions and rules without a relationship often leads to rebellion. It causes a child to lose heart (Col. 3:21). But rules within the context of a loving parent-child relationship generally lead to a positive response.

The thesis is: As parents provide the proper emotional, spiritual, and psychological stability for their child in a loving relationship, closeness will increase and the temptation to seek intimacy through sexual involvement will decrease.

What's in a Hug?

After a "Why Wait?" rally in Detroit, a girl about 14 years old came up to me with tears streaming down her face. She said, "Mr. McDowell, no one ever hugs me anymore. My dad doesn't hug me. My mom doesn't hug me—nobody."

Our study among Christian teenagers shows that 55 percent said they spent less than 15 minutes per week with their fathers! I know that as parents we have many demands on our time and that kids themselves are going in 20 different directions at once, but our kids are crying out for love and acceptance. If we don't give it to them, they may seek it elsewhere.

A 15-year-old girl wrote an essay on "What I Wish My Parents Knew about My Sexuality." Here is what she said:

I had a rotten day at school and all I wanted was a little bit of my parent's time—just a simple hug would do. But my parents both work and by the time they get home, they are usually tired and just want to be left alone. So I went to see my boyfriend and he talked to me about my problems and I felt 100 percent better. Wow! I thought, from now on I'll go to him with my problems and forget about bothering my parents. One thing has led to another and I've done things I would never have dreamed I'd do. Dad, Mom, I wish you would have been there when I needed you.

As parents, we don't have much control over the permissive attitudes of our secular society; we can't really control what our children do when they're alone on a date. But, we can control what *we* do. We can insulate our children from feeling alienated by letting them know they're accepted. We can show them our love through our words and actions—like hugs. Giving them our time sends a strong signal that they are important to us.

Information on sex, especially the reasons and benefits for waiting, is important. But the most important thing to your child is *you*. How you relate to your children—and they to you—will largely determine your ability to help them say no to sexual pressure.

It's not easy raising children in today's fast-paced society. I'm a busy parent, too. I've got places to go, audiences to speak to, books to write, and TV programs to produce. At times I feel like my life is one giant rat race. A while back, Dottie said to me, "Honey, remember, there will always be another book to write and another TV special to do, but you won't always have our five-year-old little girl to hug."

That thought has stuck with me. And since then, I have carried a letter with me from a 27-year-old woman who wrote an essay for our contest entitled "In Search of My Father's Love." Whenever I'm feeling pressured to be away from my family too much, I re-read her moving essay. It never fails to bring tears to my eyes and a renewed commitment to be there for my four darling children. Read a small portion of it with me:

When I was only 14 years of age, I dated an 18-year-old boy. I really needed his love and if the conditions to keep that love were to have sex with him, I felt I had no choice.

I felt so guilty afterwards. I can remember sobbing in my bed at night, after I'd come home from being with my boyfriend. I wanted so much to have my virginity back, and yet, it was gone—forever. I began to feel so lonely inside, but there was no one I could turn to. Certainly not my father, who would really "hate" me if he ever knew what an awful thing I had done.

After two years, I broke up with my boyfriend, but soon had another, and went through the same cycle with him. And then with another.

Isn't that ironic? The very thing I searched for—unconditional love— was being offered to me conditionally . . . "If you love me, you'll let me."

I'm 27 now, and about six months ago I wrote in my journal to the Lord, these very words . . .

"I felt lonely tonight—intense loneliness. And I realized that what I was lonely for was a 'daddy,' to be able to call him up when I hurt and hear him say he understands and to listen to me. But, I never had that with my dad. And so I am lonely without that link to my past.

"There's a song by Steve and Annie Chapman that says, 'Daddy, you're the man in your little girl's dreams, you are the one she longs to please. There's a place in her heart that can only be filled with her daddy's love. But if you don't give her the love she desires, she'll try someone else, but they won't satisfy her. . . . Don't send her away to another man's door. Nobody else can do what you do. She just needs her daddy's love.' "

Have you given your little girl her daddy's love? If you haven't please do. Go to her and tell her that you love her. And that she is the most precious girl in the world to you. And what if you think it's too late? It's never too late. Even if she's 27, it wouldn't be too late.

Josh McDowell, a popular youth speaker for Campus Crusade for Christ, has authored 28 books. His most recent book is titled *Love, Dad.*

❧ 13

Willing to Wait

A. C. Green

I've been playing ten years in the NBA, and because we travel so much, it's also hard to escape the public eye. I'm 6-foot-9, and like most basketball players, pretty easy to spot in a crowd. As a professional athlete, I have to deal with groupies in many cities. It seems as though my teammates and I are often confronted by young women wanting to meet us from the time we arrive to the time we depart. They hang out everywhere—airports, hotel lobbies, restaurants, and sports arenas—always trying to catch our eyes.

Not many resist their advances. I don't know how many virgins there are in the NBA, but you can probably count them on one hand. Pro basketball players have these larger-than-life images, and it doesn't help when a former player, such as Wilt Chamberlain, boasts about bedding 20,000 women in his lifetime.

While I've remained sexually pure, I still hear the locker-room talk about the latest sexual conquests. But I don't let that weaken my resolve, because I have chosen to follow God's standard. I've communicated my stand to my teammates. Some—in a humorous vein—have threatened to set me up with women who would make themselves available to me. "Let's see how strong you really are," they joke.

Don't get me wrong. Sex itself isn't bad. It's just a matter of *when* to experience it. God created it for enjoyment, but He also reserved it for marriage. So I'm waiting. The Bible tells me in Philippians 4:13 that "I can do all things through Christ, who strengthens me," and I've taken that verse to heart. I also know that God's Word tells me that He will not give me any temptation too great.

I want young people to hear this message. *It is possible to wait. Not everybody is doing it.* Five years years ago, I started the A. C. Green Youth Foundation in Los Angeles. We put together basketball camps, help kids find summer jobs, and try to give inner-city youths some direction. As part of that outreach, several pro athletes—Daryl Green, Barry Sanders, and David Robinson—along with a Christian rap group called Idle King, joined me to make a video called "It Ain't Worth It."

It's a rap song dealing with teenage love, broken hearts, the dilemma of abortion, and the fallacy of the "safe sex" message. We released it in 1993, and we've been able to get the video into schools and on MTV.

I would like to see more emphasis on self-control and personal responsibility in our schools. One question I ask young people is this: "Even with so much sex education being taught, why are teenage birth rates and abortion rates still so high?"

Of course, some young kids listening to me have been sexually active for years. That's when I tell them about the concept of secondary virginity. "You may have had sex in the past and think you don't have a reason to wait now," I say. "But there's a better way, and that's following God's way. Perhaps you feel guilty or not worthy, but the Lord can forgive you. After that, you can commit yourselves to remaining pure until your wedding day."

I know these kids need a role model, and while I'm reluctant to put myself on a pedestal, I will take a stand for Christ. I'm proud to say that I am a virgin, and I don't hide the strength God has given me.

You may be wondering how my message reconciles with a former teammate of mine, Magic Johnson. I think the media and society are more willing to accept Magic's message—that kids are going to have sex anyway, and the best approach is to equip them with condoms to lessen the risk of disease.

My message is different. For openers, the facts show that condoms aren't as successful as many would have you believe. And for teens, the failure rate is even worse! It's a lie to say that putting a condom on makes you as secure as Fort Knox. I cringe when I hear that stuff. Condoms have a hard enough time just stopping a woman from getting pregnant, let alone blocking an HIV virus, which is 450 times smaller than sperm itself. It's like water going through a net.

Sometimes I'm asked if have a girlfriend. Yes, I do. She really respects herself, and she has high morals and values. We share the same vision and goals, particularly when telling teens about the value of abstinence. That's what I really like telling kids: You have to learn to respect yourself before you can start respecting other people.

If you would like to contact A. C. Green, write:
A. C. Green Youth Foundation
P. O. Box 77346
Los Angeles, CA 90007

A. C. Green plays for the Phoenix Suns basketball team and lives in Los Angeles, California.

14

Hold Fast!

Patsy G. Lovell

When our second daughter, Kathleen, was 13, she was as lively as any young teenager could be. One night, she excitedly asked permission to buy a leather miniskirt, one like all the other girls in her class were wearing. As she described the benefits, I could tell she was expecting a negative response. Nonetheless, she acted surprised when I said no.

Kathleen then launched into great detail how she would be the only one in the class without a leather miniskirt. I reminded her that my answer was no and explained my reasons.

"Well, I think you're wrong!" she retorted.

"Wrong or right, I've made the decision. The answer is no."

Kathleen stomped off, but quickly turned on her heals. "I just want to explain why this is so important to me."

I nodded.

"If I don't have this miniskirt, I'll be left out, and all my friends won't like me."

113

"The answer is no," I quietly repeated.

She puffed up like a balloon and played her final card. "I thought you loved me," she wailed.

"I do. But the answer is still no."

With that, she "whumped"—a noise made only by an angry, pesky junior high kid trying to get her way. She ran upstairs and slammed her bedroom door.

Even though I had won the battle, I felt I was losing the war. I went to the living room and sat down. My husband was working late; I was the only parent "on duty." Then one of those unexplainable things happened: An inner voice said to me, *Hold fast!*

It dawned on me that Kathleen and I were not locked in a battle over a miniskirt but rather a battle of *wills*. A mother versus her 13-year-old daughter. *Hold fast* meant I needed to prevail even though I couldn't stop my hands from shaking or my stomach from churning.

The whumping noise from Kathleen's bedroom started once more, and sure enough, she appeared on the stairwell. This time, she was breathing fire.

"I thought you taught us that we have rights!" she screamed.

"You do have rights. The answer is still no."

She wound up again, but I cut her off. "Kathleen, I have made my decision. I will not change my mind, and if you say another word about this, you will be severely punished. Now go to bed!"

She still had a few words left, but she held them in check. She loped off to bed, still seething.

I sat on the couch, shaking and upset. None of the children had ever pushed me so far. I leafed through a book, too wound up to go to bed. Just when I thought our skirmishes were over, the sound of whumping came again. Kathleen came down the stairs.

"Well," she announced, "I'm just going to tell you one more time. . . ."

I met her at the bottom step, planted my hands on my hips, and looked her in the eyes. "Do not answer," I said. "Do not say yes or no. Do not say anything. Do not say 'Yes, ma'am' or 'No, ma'am.' Turn around and go to bed. And do not make a single sound!"

She slowly turned and trudged upstairs without a word. I dropped onto the couch, thoroughly exhausted.

For several minutes I stared into space and wondered what my blood pressure count was. Then I heard her door open. Kathleen, her nose and eyes red from crying, walked down the stairs in pajamas. Curlers were in her hair. She held out her hands to me.

"Oh, Mom, I'm sorry."

We hugged as she said through her tears, "I was *so* scared!"

"Scared of what?"

"I was scared that you were going to let me win!" she sniffed.

You were scared that I was going to let you win? I was perplexed for a moment. Then I realized that my daughter had wanted *me* to win!

I had held fast, and she was convinced I had done what a mother needed to do. Her simple words gave me the reassurance I needed.

Children love their parents, but they cannot handle being equal with them. Deep down, they do not see themselves as grown up. In fact, they will, if they can get away with it, bring a parent down to their level, so that all the family seems like a group of kids.

Deep down, teens know they need guidance and leadership. Parents, it's up to us to give it to them.

Remember: *Hold fast!*

Patsy Lovell is a middle school teacher in Hazel Green, Alabama.

15

Can I Have the Car Keys Friday Night?

Sandra Picklesimer Aldrich

O ne Saturday afternoon last fall, I came home from the store just as my son, Jay, then 17, and four friends arrived from a school activity. The young men deposited the groceries on the kitchen counter and gladly wolfed down a platter of brownies.

Just then, my 16-year-old daughter, Holly, walked into the kitchen. One young man cheerfully greeted her. She smiled, then turned to me.

"Mom, Jim's the one who's helping me in math class."

"So, you're Holly's Big Brother," I chirped.

As Jim returned a polite smile, I could see Jay in the hallway slapping his forehead. Later, he told me the guys really razzed Jim, making stabbing gestures toward their hearts.

"But what did I say?" I asked, bewildered. "I thought I was giving him a compliment."

Jay put his hand on my shoulder in that way teens have of letting mothers know they've missed the mark.

"Mom, that's a put-down now, especially if the guy likes the girl as much as Jim likes Holly."

What? Jim *likes* Holly? Wait a minute. I taught high school for 15 years in the Detroit area. I know teens. I *like* teens. And communication with my two kids is a top priority. So how'd I get out of touch with what was going on? I took another look at my rosy-cheeked daughter and decided I'd better find out—fast.

Taking Notes

That night over pizza at our favorite restaurant, I peppered my kids with questions.

"When we lived in New York," I began, "you said it was customary for a guy to ask the girl out, and as soon as she'd accept the date, they'd kiss. Does that happen here, too?"

Both shrugged. "Sometimes."

I gulped but tried to keep the panic out of my voice. "That ever happen to you?"

Holly rolled her eyes. "Mom! No!"

I relaxed—just a little bit—and, for the next hour, listened as they gave me an overview of what was happening at their school. Casual dating is now called "seeing each other," while what I once called "going steady" is merely "going out."

The angora wool that the girl of my day wrapped around her boyfriend's ring each night—to make it fit her own finger—is as outdated as malt-shop waitresses on roller skates.

"Do kids still exchange class rings?" I asked.

Holly shook her head. "Not much. The guy's mother always says, 'I didn't pay that much for a ring just to have some girl lose it.' So girls wear them during school—if at all—and then on a chain. Most of the time, though, the girl wears her boyfriend's varsity jacket all day. Now *that's* great."

Those casual remarks soon gave way to descriptions of "outer-wear" (frilly bras and girdles worn as public attire), classmates' heavy necking between classes, and the principal's annual letter asking parents not to rent hotel rooms for their child's prom night. As a single mom (my husband, Don, died nine years ago), I was rapidly deciding that the best years for me were when Jay was 15 and Holly 14—because he couldn't drive and she couldn't date!

Talking with the Experts

In the days that followed, I thought a lot about our talk. I was already praying for my teens, so what else could I do to make sure they didn't succumb to all those temptations? I decided to ask folks who could give me some insight into the modern family.

Darrell Pearson, director of youth ministries at First Presbyterian Church in Colorado Springs (where the kids and I attend church), has worked with teens since 1981. I anticipated advice for parents to keep their children active in church. Darrell surprised me.

"Parenthood doesn't come with guarantees, even if we do all the 'right' things," said Darrell. "But if we remember that we are stewards of our children—that they belong to God and not to us—we'll see our responsibilities better. Most youngsters don't need *more* activities; they need time with their parents. But today's lifestyles makes that difficult even—and maybe especially—for church families because they already have so many responsibilities outside the home."

My next call was to Paul Ardelean Jr., alumni director and former dean of students at Bryan College in Dayton, Tennessee.

"I'm convinced many Christian students have the same problems as non-Christians," he said. "They take their moral standards from movies and TV instead of the Bible. They don't know how to date and get to know each other. Often they date once and immediately establish inappropriate commitments. They accept abortion and aren't concerned about AIDS because they think it'll never happen to them.

"Parents must *train* their children as well as commit them to the Lord. But they opt out of their responsibility, thinking they'll just put them into a Christian school. Many young people are already emotionally needy when they enroll."

Then I reached Carl Amann, a high school counselor in Garden City, Michigan, who has worked with teens for nearly three decades. When I asked what he sees as the biggest problem in today's family, he didn't hesitate. "No one answers to anyone," he said. "Even in our little community, we have 80 percent of our students living with only one natural parent. Once I asked my students, 'How many of you have a seat at the dinner table that you call your own?' Only a couple kids raised their hands. They go home, grab something for supper, and eat while they watch TV.

"The family doesn't talk—even if they're home together. So where can the teen go to ask questions about moral issues? Parents need to be available. And kids need to know they can ask questions. They talk to me because there's very little communication in the home."

Applying the Knowledge

As I listened to the advice, I thought of my own former students who had made inappropriate and even tragic choices over the years. Jay and Holly had grown up hearing my admonishments that they were to live in a way they wouldn't regret later. More than once I'd told them about the girls who've given in to sexual pressure and then sobbed to me, "I want to go back to the way I was."

My kids had gotten this far without serious problems, so maybe they'd listened more than I thought. But we were in a new setting in Colorado Springs, and I couldn't make assumptions about the standards of new friends. It was time to take drastic action, especially with the boys lining up to ask Holly out. Thus, I started a routine known as The Talk.

The Talk consists of having Holly's would-be date answer pleasantly asked questions such as "How long have you lived in this area? "What do your folks do?" and "Do you have brothers and sisters? Within a few minutes, the questions advance to "What are you planning to study in college?" "What church does your family attend?" and "Do you have time to be very active in your church youth group?"

The first young man answered the opening questions politely but kept glancing toward the stairway, wondering when Holly would be ready.

I smiled. "It's okay. She'll be downstairs when this is over."

I settled comfortably into the sofa corner. "Even though we met a couple of weeks ago, I didn't know anything about you before we began this chat," I said. "Right now you think this is ridiculous, but I guarantee you that in about 25 years when a guy asks your future daughter out, you'll think of me and say, 'That ol' lady was right!' "

I let that thought sink in. Then I continued. "I know you two are just going out as friends, but I've lived long enough to know how quickly situations can change. So remember this, treat Holly the way you hope some other guy is treating your future wife."

His eyes widened at that thought. I knew I'd hit my target.

Since my first "Talk," word's gotten around school. Now when a new guy hints he'd like to ask Holly out, the others warn him about The Talk.

Only one young man has refused to meet with me. Holly told him not to call her again. "It's like my mom says, 'You don't have to like it; you just have to do it,' " she said.

She later confessed she was glad I had the rule because the guy was actually "kinda creepy" anyway. How I appreciated her saying that.

Helping Our Teens Say No

Those talks with Holly's dates—as traumatic as they are for all of us—are almost easy compared with the conversations I've had with Jay about his dating. Remember the days when the mothers had to teach their daughters to say no? Well, the mother of the '90s is having to teach her *son* to refuse advances, too.

When one of the women in my Bible study group described a breathy, suggestive message a 17-year-old had left on her answering machine, another mother topped it with an account of her son's girlfriend wanting their prom night to be "just like our wedding night."

Anyway, here are a few things we've learned to make this time in life less stressful:

• *Expect your teen to have high standards.* I'm saddened by the number of parents who *expect* their sons to be sexually active even in this day of rampant out-of-wedlock conceptions and sexually transmitted diseases. Teens often hear from their peers that they can be a "real man" for fathering a child. As adults we need to set high standards for our children—through our words as well as our actions—and let them know that *real* men and women do not act irresponsibly.

I've found that when adults say, "Be careful that your feelings don't run away with you," they're conveying the idea that sexual feelings are so strong they can overrule judgment. That's an incorrect message to give.

Sexual feelings don't have to be acted on any more than feelings of anger. One mother left this message on a three-by-five card in her teens' rooms: "You may not be able to control your feelings, but you *can* control your actions."

• *Express trust in your teen.* I remember more than one student who grumbled, "If my mom's gonna accuse me of it, I might as well do it."

When Karen's 19-year-old son was home for semester break, he mentioned that his girlfriend was pressuring him to spend the weekend at her parents' cabin. Karen wanted to scream, "She's a hussy!" But she took a deep breath, reminded him he knew that was wrong, and then managed to say, "No matter how difficult it is, I know you'll always make the right choice." Her son later said her trust gave him the strength to break off the relationship.

• *Anticipate problems.* Even while you're trusting your teen, you can't close your eyes to potentially dangerous situations. Most of us managed to survive the sexual temptations of our own early years because we were supported by a society, church, and family that shouted, "No!" and "Wait!"

Today, teens are hearing a different message from those same institutions—along with the media's siren call: "If it feels good, just do it." They need us to say, "No, you're not going there if the parents aren't home."

• *Talk with your teen.* Don't assume you know what's going on. In a non-threatening way, ask if anything is troubling him or her about the relationship.

Amy noticed that her 17-year-old son was withdrawing from family activities. One Saturday morning, over a leisurely pancake breakfast, she asked if he wished he could change anything.

"You bet, Mom," he said. "I wish I were older so Sheila and I could get married."

With all the calmness and candor she could muster, Amy talked to him about the sexual pressures he was facing and decided that the best way to help was by including his girlfriend in more of their family activities so they could spend time together without the temptations of intense dating.

• *Get to know your teen's date.* Think of the young man or woman not as the enemy but as a potential friend and even future in-law. When Lynn's son, Paul, started seriously dating a non-Christian, Lynn knew she'd drive him away if she harangued him with admonishments about being "unequally yoked together."

Instead, while she patiently reminded Paul of God's concern for the future, she welcomed the girl and lovingly worked at getting to know her. As the opportunities arose, she even shared her faith, explaining why it was so important. Because the young woman felt so comfortable with Lynn, she readily consented to attend church with the family. Two weeks before the young couple got engaged, Lynn had the privilege of leading her future daughter-in-law to the Lord.

My son, Jay, is in college this year, so I'm no longer involved in his every dating situation. But while I can't counsel him before he goes out the door, I know my prayers have more power than my talks. So, believe me, I pray *a lot*.

As parents—and especially as single moms—we may not get through this stage as well as we'd like, but by talking to our children, keeping them in a good youth group, and being ever watchful, we increase our chances of raising them to make sound moral choices.

Isn't that the goal of every parent?

Some of this material is adapted from the book *From One Single Mother to Another*, by Sandra P. Aldrich. Copyright © 1991. Regal Books, Ventura, California 93003. Used by permission.

16

Charting a Different Course

Mike Yorkey

One afternoon after school, a sophomore lad slipped into Christi Ham's classroom.

Visibly distraught, the boy stood near the door. Mrs. Ham, a religion teacher at Pacelli High in Columbus, asked the student to sit down and compose himself.

"I can't stand it," he said in a choked voice, as the teacher patted his shoulder. "I can't fight the pressure anymore."

Gently, Mrs. Ham asked what was bothering him. Was he having trouble with his girlfriend? Was it the pressure to party and drink?

"No," the boy replied. "It's all the pressure *not* to drink."

In a flash, Mrs. Ham understood. Because of a peer counseling group on campus called Teen Advisers, drinking was no longer cool at Pacelli (pronounced *Puh-CHELL-eee*). The sophomore, who liked to down beer at weekend parties, was tired of hearing his class-mates tell him to abstain from alcohol.

The Pacelli Teen Advisers—and similar groups around the country—have turned peer pressure into a positive force. The message not to drink or do drugs is coming from the students themselves—not parents and school officials, a concept that makes the Teen Advisers so interesting.

The Columbus program began in 1987 when Richard and Dee Dee Stephens' eldest daughter, Mary Lawson (that's her first and middle name), was attending Pacelli, a Catholic high school with more than half of its students coming from Protestant denominations.

Back then, every weekend was marked by bitter arguments between daughter and parents. Why? Mary Lawson wasn't allowed to go out to parties. A popular cheerleader, she yearned to be accepted by the "in crowd," but that crowd usually huddled around a beer keg every Friday and Saturday night.

As Christian parents, Richard and Dee Dee wanted to do something *pro-active* about the peer pressure. They were convinced that if several high school students would take a stand against drinking, drugs, and premarital sex, more would follow. In addition, they were sure impressionable freshmen and junior high students would readily listen to upperclassmen.

That spring, Dee Dee and another mother, Kit Newlin, asked the principal of a Columbus-area junior high if they and several students could talk to an eighth-grade class about dating. The moms were joined by four Pacelli High students, including Mary Lawson (who came around to her parents' point of view) and Kit's daughter, Missy. They answered questions the eighth-graders had written anonymously on three-by-five cards.

The first panel was so well received that Dee Dee telephoned eight more students and asked if *they* would be interested in talking to junior-highers about drinking.

Dee Dee mentioned one little catch, however: The teens had to agree not to drink for the rest of the school year. "I asked another junior whom I *knew* was drinking to take the pledge," remembers Dee Dee. "I knew if she would do it, 10 kids would follow her. She said yes, and since then, I've found that more kids will take this step if they know their friends are going to stand with them."

Then Dee Dee and Kit accompanied the dozen students to a PRIDE (Parents' Resource Instate for Drug Education) workshop in Atlanta where they heard about a Teen Adviser program developed by Diane Chenoweth and Syd Schnaars for Olentangy High School, a public school in Delaware, Ohio. Dee Dee purchased a manual and went to work tailoring a Christian-based program to fit the needs of Pacelli's 400 students.

"Sitting at that conference, it was like lightning struck," says Dee Dee. "I *knew* it could work in our area, too. Just before school started, Richard and I put the word out, and 42 students agreed to attend a weekend retreat to kick off the school year."

At the retreat, the Stephenses organized games and activities that brought the students closer together, much like a summer football camp. "By Saturday night, the kids had really jelled as a team," recalls Dee Dee, "and they wanted to go out and make a difference in their school. On Sunday afternoon, she and Richard presented the teens with contracts stipulation that they would not drink alcohol, take drugs, or use tobacco products for one year.

When Mary Lawson inked her pact, she received a dose of self-confidence to stand against negative peer pressure. "I made a commitment that I knew I had to live up to," she says. "And I did."

These days, the Teen Advisers program has spread all across the country as parents have learned about Pacelli High's success story. And just before he left office, President Bush presented the Stephens with the 987th "Point of Light" award in a White House ceremony.

Learning More

As Teen Advisers has grown, so has its scope. They meet at least one Sunday afternoon a month at the Stephens' home to talk about how to avoid drinking, sexual pressure, getting along with parents, and the importance of self-esteem.

But the main purpose of Teen Advisers is their work with the Pacelli freshmen class, who are excluded from joining the group. Several times a month, the upperclassmen meet with freshmen classes by leading small groups that precipitate more intimate discussions.

"Our seniors and juniors," says Dee Dee, "are saying to the younger students, 'Hey, we've been there, and we're going to tell you what it's like *not* to drink and *not* to get physical with your boyfriend or girlfriend.' When you're a freshman, you will listen to someone two years older, even more so than your parents."

In a way, this arrangement sets up an unexpected system of accountability. How? A Teen Adviser *knows* the freshmen are watching him closely to see if he backs up his word.

But what happens if a Teen Adviser stumbles and parties hearty? "If you know someone who breaks the contract, you're bound to go to that person and ask him to turn himself in," says Rusty Walker, a Pacelli senior. "If that doesn't work, you're supposed to turn him in yourself. If you don't, then you've broken *your* contract."

Teens who have slipped up appear before the Teen Adviser Honor Council, a panel of six elected by other TAs. Notice again that accountability is coming from teen to teen. (Although Teen Advisers espouse abstinence, sexual purity is not part of the contract because the teens didn't feel comfortable discussing the sex lives of their friends.)

"We want those who have broken their contract to be honest," explains Rusty, who's also an Honor Council member. "If they are sorry and want to remain with the group, they have to apologize to all the Teen Advisers. They also have to tell their parents—perhaps the toughest part of all. Then they are given a punishment, which is usually a Saturday afternoon of community service."

Another student, Becky Davidson, says signing the contract is a big commitment. "It's not fun and games. Even if there had ever been times when I wanted to break my contract, I wouldn't have because not only had I signed it before other teens, I had signed it before God."

Back to School

It's a Monday morning in Mrs. Rivard's eighth-grade class at St. Anne's, a parochial junior high school. This is the first class of the day for the 13-and 14-year-old students, who are dressed in their blue-and-yellow school uniforms. Ten Teen Advisers walk in and sit before the students. Mrs. Rivard introduces the group, then adds, "The Teen Advisers are here to talk to you about drinking and to answer the questions you wrote out last week."

The eighth-graders appear excited, but they also take pains to be cool. They don't notice Dee Dee slipping into the back of the classroom, where she monitors all the Teen Advisers' panels.

The TAs are given permission by Pacelli to miss class several times a month to speak before various junior high classes in the Columbus area. Because of the success of the Pacelli program, school authorities recognize that the Teen Advisers reach younger students in ways adults never will.

"Drinking—and the pressure to drink—is one of the top problems facing teenagers today," begins Randi Dean, a senior. "And alcohol is the most widely used drug," chips in cheerleader Kristie Wheeler. "It kills more people than any other drug."

Several other TAs pick up the beat. "The younger you are when you start drinking, the greater the chances you'll become an alcoholic," says Adam Conard. "After an adult starts drinking, it can take five to 15 years to become an alcoholic. Once a teenager starts drinking, it can take only six to 18 *months* to become an alcoholic."

Rusty Walker says everyone on the panel has taken a firm stand against drinking, noting that all the Teen Advisers had signed one-year contracts not to drink alcohol.

"When you get to Pacelli," Rusty tells the rapt eighth-graders, "don't plan on drinking beer if you want to be cool. That won't be the way to go. You know those beer commercials with the hard-body guys and Swedish bikini teams? Well, those aren't the usual drinkers. A beer drinker is usually a couch potato with a big beer belly."

The eighth-graders giggle, and then one raises his hand. "Have you ever had anything to drink?" he asks.

Nearly everyone on the panel nods yes. Most say they tried beer or hard liquor at a friend's party while they were in junior high. One girl says her mom offered her sips of bacardi rum while the family was vacationing in Florida. "Imagine having the pressure to drink from your parents!"

Dee Dee leans over to a visitor. "Four years ago, when Teen Advisers heard this question, they usually answered, "I was getting drunk last year, but now I'm not." Now, it's 'I had a beer back in junior high.' That's how I have seen the pendulum swing in just five years."

Talking about S-E-X

The last time the Teen Advisers did a "sex panel," they received a cool reception at a Columbus public school eighth-grade class.

The eighth-graders may have listened to the Teen Advisers' pro-abstinence message, but they weren't buying it. When the TAs talked about the consequences of an unplanned pregnancy, one eighth-grader raised her hand and described her 17-year-old sister's pregnancy and safe delivery of a little boy. The father married the sister, she said, and they were doing just fine.

It was a "take-that" statement hurled at the panel. Jennifer Young remembers being taken aback for a moment, but after a quick, silent prayer, she plunged ahead. "I am really happy that it worked out for your sister," she said, "but she's an exception. She's maybe the one out of 100 that works out, but for the other 99, their lives are ruined." She also told the eighth-grader it's okay not to do it, that she's a virgin, and she is going to save herself until marriage.

The Teen Advisers continued that "wait-until-marriage" theme at another sex panel before a seventh-grade class at St. Anne's. "We want to tell y'all that safe sex is sex with the person you marry," began Shawn Scott, a senior.

The Teen Advisers then shared statistics about the low effectiveness rate of condoms and the danger of AIDS and sexually transmitted diseases. "And there's no condom that protects your heart, your mind, and your self-esteem," said Lauren Jones. "When you start having sex, pretty soon that's all you'll have in common. You can't go back to kissing because sex is progressive."

The panel then entertained questions from the seventh-graders:

- *"How far should you go on the first date?"* Their answer: Although it's expected to kiss on the first date, you certainly don't have to, the panel agreed. Anne Stephens, a junior and one of Dee Dee's three daughters, said she went with a guy for four months before they kissed. "That made it a lot more special."

- *"When should I start dating?"* You should talk it over with your parents, the panelists replied. Group dates are the best because that won't put you in a compromising position.

- *"Should I go out with a guy even if I don't like him?"* Shawn took this one. "Guys don't want 'pity dates,' " he said. "You'll both end up having a lousy time."

The strapping, six-foot, 180-pound Shawn then turned the discussion to premarital sex. "I'm 18, and I'm a virgin, so don't let people out there tell you no one's a virgin anymore," he said. The seventh-graders didn't make a sound as they hung onto his words. "I think being a virgin makes me more of a man. It takes more character and more will power *not* to have sex these days."

The Generations Meet

An important part of Teen Advisers is the once-a-quarter Parents' Night. With 80 parents seated in the Pacelli auditorium, Dee Dee began the evening by describing the world in which today's high school students are growing up: 10 percent of teens are alcoholics; two out of every 10 unmarried teen girls become pregnant (and half of them abort); date rape is a common problem on college campuses; and teens are committing suicide in higher numbers than ever before.

Then Dee Dee told the parents that she asked the TAs at a previous meeting to write a paragraph—anonymously—to their parents. They were to pretend that this would be their last communication with their parents.

Dee Dee read several to the attentive parents, some complimentary, some poignant:

> *There are so many things I have to tell you. I am so sorry for all the pain I have caused you. I was mean, selfish, and hateful. I'm not proud of that. I thought I was always right; I have told you I hated you often. But if I were a parent, I would do things just the way you have done them.*
>
> *I know I'm not the easiest person in the world to get along with. But it always seems that you somehow accept me for who I am. I really respect you for not giving up on me. I love you and pray to God that I will carry the morals and values you have taught me.*
>
> *I've always loved you, yet you have treated me like an outsider. I wish you could include me, trust me, and be my friend. I'm not as horrible as you think I am. I wish I could be given a chance.*

Happy Days

As Parents' Night came to a close, several fathers spoke up about Teen Advisers. "When my boys went to Pacelli 15 years ago," said Joe Wheeler, "it was: 'Who can spin the most doughnuts in the parking lot and drink the most beer?' My oldest son was the class president, and it took him 15 years to get off Skoal chewing tobacco. He started chewing when he was on the football team because it was the macho thing to do in those days. He didn't quit until the birth of his first child.

"You should see this school now," continued Joe. "It's as calm as can be, like back in the '50s. Fifteen years ago, if a boy stood up and said he was a virgin, they would have laughed him out of the school.

"What I like is that Kristie, my sophomore daughter, is getting a good education. She doesn't have to worry about all this drinking and drugs stuff. Yup, this school has really turned around."

Mike Yorkey is a former newspaper editor who became editor of *Focus on the Family* magazine in 1986. Mike is the general editor of *Growing a Healthy Home*, a compilation of articles from *Focus on the Family* magazine. Mike and his wife, Nicole, and two children, Andrea and Patrick, live in Colorado Springs, Colorado.

17

Dressed to Impress

Becky Foster Still

Sixteen-year-old Tim Miller had his eye on a pair of new sneakers. He knew his parents would spend $50, but anything beyond that would have to come from his paper route earnings. So he saved his money, combed the local mall for a pair of Insta-Pump Shaq Attaq IIIs and finally spotted some in his size. The price tag for these Reebok athletic shoes—$145, pump included.

In Albuquerque, 12-year-old Lisa Farmington wants a Guess? jeans-and-jacket outfit, but mom Janet simply can't afford the $100-plus cost. "I did buy her the Espirit book bag all the other kids have," she says, "but this is beginning to get out of hand!"

Wearing the "right" clothes has always been important to young people. In the '60s, it was go-go boots and fringe jackets. In the '70s, bell-bottoms and Earth shoes. In the '80s, Lycra stretch pants and neon colors. So what's different now?

In our materialistic times, the obsession with clothes has escalated to new heights. Not only do young people feel peer pressure to wear the right style, but it must be the right *label*: Bugle Boy, Guess?, Nike, Reebok, Espirit, Stussy, Bennetton, or Cavarrichi, to name a few.

And those desired labels are more expensive than ever. Ann Foster of Loveland, Colorado, took her 10-year-old son shopping for sneakers recently, but the trip was fruitless. "Steven wanted a pair that cost $69.95, so we came home with no shoes at all," she says. "And he thought he was being fair by staying out of the $100 range!"

Something else new is that boys have become as picky as girls—not only about *what* they buy, but *where* they shop. Fourteen-year-old Steve Jackson teasingly calls his younger sister a "KSS"—K Mart shoe shopper—and that's certainly not meant as a compliment.

His mom, Carol, says she can easily take Steve to three or four stores before he finds exactly what he wants. "Shopping is an exhausting experience for him," she says, "because he gets stressed about finding something his friends will approve of."

The other bad news is that kids are becoming more clothes-conscious at increasingly younger ages. Ann Foster says many of her son's fourth-grade classmates wear Nikes that retail for $100 and up. "And you know they don't last very long," she adds. "You and I can wear shoes for a while, but these kids grow out of them in no time!"

Peers Are Ruthless

Wander onto a school campus these days, and it may seem that students haven't put much thought into the clothes they're wearing. Jeans, shorts, baggy pants, casual shirts, and athletic shoes are the order of the day. "Kids are definitely dressing down compared to previous generations," says Joe Fox, principal of Dana Junior High School in Arcadia, California.

What an outsider may not realize is that much thought *has* gone into these outfits. Why? Because the "in crowd" can be ruthless.

Clothes without the right labels are jeeringly called "bo-bos," "no names" or "fish heads."

Younger children don't hesitate to make fun of classmates who aren't dressed appropriately. "If you're wearing just plain jeans and a T-shirt, the kids wearing Cavarrichis will say 'You're not cool,'" says one Florida girl in sixth grade. "Or they just look at you in a way that means, 'Oh, disgusting!'"

Among older kids, the pressure is more subtle. "I think my friends will accept me more if I'm wearing something like Espirit or Generra," says Christine, a high school sophomore. "It's not something we talk about, but it's definitely there."

In addition, most kids can be sure their peers are noticing how often they're wearing various outfits. Diane Langberg, a psychologist in Philadelphia, Pennsylvania, hears such comments from her 11-year-old son. "His friends let him know if they've seen things too often," she says.

All of this adds up to stress for today's schoolchildren that goes way beyond the normal pressures of completing homework and passing exams. "I think about what I'm going to wear the whole day before," says one Southern California teen. She confides that she even keeps a calendar of her outfits, making sure she doesn't wear the same thing more than once every two weeks.

The clothing obsession has a dark side, too. At some schools, especially those in the inner city, students deal drugs to finance the top-of-the-line shoes and jackets they want. Gangs often claim a particular item of clothing as a "trademark" to identify themselves. Worst of all, cities such as Baltimore and Chicago have seen incidents of clothes-motivated killings among students.

These are the extreme cases, however. It's not a brand-name jungle everywhere; some schools and area are harder hit with the fashion obsession than others. Factors such as a school's size, location, relative affluence, and "cliquishness" contribute to the extent of the problem.

Why the Problem?

Despite the regional differences, just about every school has seen more clothing competitiveness in recent years. Who's to blame?

The media, many say. Television and print advertising subtly influences all of us to some degree. But kids, at the most impressionable and emotionally vulnerable stage of their lives, are especially susceptible to its lure.

With their fragile egos, teens and preteens are easily convinced they simply are not with it if they don't wear a certain label. And advertisements that target young people use the image angle to the hilt, selling the attractiveness of a lifestyle rather than the functions of a product.

But it's too easy to use the media as a scapegoat, others say. "Frankly, I think some parents buy their kids expensive things as a substitute for their time and affection," says one Colorado schoolteacher. "And lots of times when you see a status-quo child, a status-conscious parent is behind the scene."

The Ultimate Dress Code

Whatever the underlying reasons, too many youngsters today spend more time studying one another's pant-seat label than their math and English books. Few would disagree these kids should be channeling their energy into more constructive areas: academics, sports, friends, and family. So where's the answer?

Some public schools have adopted a dramatic solution: uniforms. Traditionally used only at private schools, uniforms have now been introduced in Baltimore, Detroit, Miami, Washington, Philadelphia, and New Orleans. Dozens of school districts are examining the concept.

At first, most students—especially older ones—aren't wild about this because they feel it infringes on their individuality and freedom of expression. But in the schools that have adopted uniforms, a majority of students do decide to wear them—even though all public-school uniform programs are voluntary.

Parents, teachers, and students alike claim that rather than restricting individual expression, the prescribed outfits actually give pupils *more* freedom to be themselves—because they're not being judged by the labels on their jeans.

"Before, some of the kids who had better clothes would act as though they were better than other people," says Wendy Diaz, a uniform wearer in Miami.

Eliminating the whole issue of clothing competitiveness also allows students to concentrate more on scholastic interest, and school administrators believe it promotes discipline. "Before we had uniforms, I spent an inordinate amount of time dealing with little squabbles that cropped up about who was wearing what," says Melody Martin, principal of Damon J. Keith Elementary in Detroit.

Adds Miami principal Lottie Downie, "I've always believed if you dress as though you're going to the beach, you act as though you're at the beach." And uniforms don't have to be drab and unattractive. "Ours are neat, they're smart-looking, and the kids like them," says Downie.

Negotiating the Clothes Wars

If you are fighting a fashion battle with your youngster, consider some of the following suggestions:

• **How about uniforms?** If you think a uniform program—appropriate especially at the grade-school level—might work at *your* child's school, bring it up with the principal. In many of the public schools that now have uniforms, concerned parents lobbied for the idea.

• **Look at your own lifestyle.** Think about the messages getting through to your children about the relative importance of image and consumption. Although this point may seem obvious, it's all too easy for us to model behavior we don't really want our children to imitate. How do you and your spouse make spending decisions for the family? How do you think your children would describe your priorities?

• **Help your children understand the principle of limited resources.** It's never too early to teach your youngsters about the value of money and the need to budget for clothes.

Many parents have solved their clothing disputes by setting definite amounts they'll pay for wardrobe items, with any additional cost having to come from the youngster's own earnings. "When my daughter saw how much she would have to work to pay for the outfits she wanted, she suddenly didn't want them as much," says one San Diego mother.

• **Remember who's in control.** "Parents must be able to say 'no' when their children make unreasonable demands for clothes," comments Principal Fox. In all aspects of child raising—including wardrobe standoffs—you'll have times when you, as a parent, must exercise your authority. Decide what your budget can afford, communicate clear guidelines to your youngsters, and resist manipulation games.

• **Use balance.** Be firm but understanding. Discuss the clothing issue openly with your kids. Educate yourself on what kids are wearing at school, and be fair in setting your limits. Remember that peer pressure is an undeniable presence for *every* generation of young people.

"You have to be sensitive to the fact you're talking about very fragile self-esteems," says psychologist Langberg in Philadelphia. "There has to be some alikeness to peers or the child will be hurt, because kids can be brutal to one another!"

• **Be resourceful.** If your teen just has to have brand names, keep your eye out for good deals. Label clothing *does* go on sale, and many say they can find reasonably priced Guess? jeans or Espirit shirts at discount stores and factory outlets.

But we can't deny it: Peer pressure can be overwhelming. Remember Tim Miller, the young lad who carefully squirreled away his paper route money to buy a pair of Shaq Attaq III's? Believe it or not, he reconsidered his purchase for a couple of weeks—all because a friend said he thought $145 was too much to pay.

In the end, though, the greater kind of peer pressure won out. Tim went back to the store, forked over his hard-won earnings, and walked out with a shoebox full of leather, rubber, and status.

But will he still be wearing his Shaqs six months from now, when Dennis Rodman's Darwin shoes from Nike become the next footwear fashion rage?

Becky Foster Still lives in Southern California and has a daughter, Emilie. So far, Becky has resisted buying Guess? jeans for Emilie.

18

A Promise with a Ring to It

Richard Durfield

With a flourish, the hostess seated my son, Jonathan, and me in El Encanto's main dining room, a nice restaurant in the foothills near our hometown. The expensive furnishings, subdued lighting, and pricy menu told my 15-year-old that tonight was a special occasion.

Jonathan is the youngest of four children. As we scanned the large red menus, I mentally walked through what I wanted to say to him. He knew we were at El Encanto's for his "key talk," a time when we could discuss any questions he had about sexuality. Jonathan already knew the "facts of life"—my wife, Renee, and I had raised him in a home where "no question is too dumb." We began telling him about sexual parts in his preschool days. Last year,

Jonathan took a ninth-grade health class on human reproduction.

But this night would go beyond anatomy to talk about the special meaning of commitment and honor for a young man fast growing up. When the chilled jumbo shrimp appetizers arrived at our table, I quietly leaned over.

"Tonight is your night, Jonathan," I began. "This is a special time for you and Dad to talk about any sexual questions that might still be on your mind. Whatever might seem a little awkward at times, well, tonight is the right time to ask. Nothing is off limits tonight.

"If something's been bothering you about adolescence or whatever, it's okay to talk about it. As we eat through the course of the evening, I want you to just be thinking about any questions you might have."

Jonathan's all boy. He'd much rather ride his mountain bike in the hills than chase after girls. When we first sat down, he had seemed a little uncomfortable because I saw him looking around. But as we began talking, he relaxed a bit.

My son, who has never been on a date, wanted to know *for sure* what "the line" was. How far was *too far*? He had a good idea, but he wanted to hear it from me.

"A light kiss is about as far as you can go," I replied. "Sexual emotions are very strong, and if you're not careful, you'll do things you don't want to. So you need to avoid anything that leads you up to that."

For instance, I explained, certain types of kissing are going too far. Kissing a girl on the neck can lead to going much further.

The "Key Talk" Beginnings

Jonathan has two older sisters and one brother: Kimberli, 23, Anna, 19, and Tim, 18. About 10 years ago, when Kimberli was entering adolescence, Renee and I had an idea: have a private, personal, and intimate time with the child to explain conception, the biblical view of marriage, and the sacredness of sexual purity. A time with a mom and daughter or a dad and son can candidly discuss the questions, fears, and anxieties of adolescence. I called it a "key talk."

We also had another idea. At the time of the key talk, the parent presents a specially made "key" ring to the son or daughter. The ring, which symbolizes a commitment with God, is worn by the adolescent during the difficult teen and young adult years.

What is a key ring? The purpose of a key is to unlock a door, and the ring symbolizes the key to one's heart and virginity. The ring is a powerful reminder of the value and beauty of virginity, of the importance of reserving sex for marriage.

The ring also represents a covenant between the child and God. A covenant not only obligates us to God, but it obligates God to us. As long as we honor a covenant, God will also honor it. Throughout history, God has blessed those who have remained faithful.

The son or daughter wears the key ring until he or she is married. Then the ring is taken off and presented to the new spouse on their wedding night—that sacred evening when a life of sexual experience begins.

Renee had open and frank key talks with Kimberli and Anna. She described just about everything a child would want to know about sex. Because our daughters are attractive, intelligent, and sought-after, they needed important reasons to remain virgins until their wedding nights.

The pressure of society and its "well, they're going to do it anyway" attitude pushes millions of teenagers into a world of promiscuity. Sadly, our daughters are members of a shrinking minority: less than 50 percent of women 18 and younger are virgins. And churched kids are having sex in nearly the same percentages as non-churched kids.

Jonathan's Ring

As the main dishes were taken away, I told Jonathan it was time to make a commitment before the Lord. Yes, we lacked privacy, but I felt it added to the significance of what he was about to do.

I wanted Jonathan to pray—right there at the table—but I had to set things up a little bit. "Now this covenant is going to be something between you and God until you are married," I said. "We're going to include whoever your wife will be in this prayer. We're going to ask God that wherever she is and whoever she is, that He'll be with her also. We'll ask Him to help her to be chaste until the time you're married. I want you to ask God for His grace to keep this covenant pure, because even though you may have right intentions, sometimes things go wrong. I want you to pray and then Dad will pray."

Jonathan turned to me and took my hands. It surprised me that he would be so bold in a public restaurant, but I realized that was exactly what he needed in order to stand alone.

Jonathan bowed his head and prayed fervently. Then it was my turn. Before I prayed, I said, "Jonathan, I have something for you." I took a custom-made 14K ring and slipped it on his finger. Bowing our heads, I asked the Lord to honor the covenant Jonathan was making and help him resist temptation in the coming years.

Then I read a letter from someone very special, someone who had befriended Jonathan when he was much younger. I didn't let him know who it was from:

> Dear Jonathan,
>
> Your dad told me that the two of you are about to have a very important talk. I've been invited to participate in the discussion by way of a letter. I was asked to say a few things about purity—sexual purity—though I don't suppose there's much I can tell you that you haven't heard before.
>
> I'm sure your parents have taught you well. But I want to encourage you to act on what you already know. Believe me, it's worth it to save sex for marriage and keep yourself pure for the woman God wants you to spend you life with. The Lord designed it that way for good reason. Plenty of people who disregarded His plan in that area will tell you how much they regret it.
>
> You're going to need more of this kind of encouragement in the days to come. It's one thing to know what's right. Living

by it is something else. Over the next few years, you'll probably face pressure to change or compromise your values— pressure from your friends, from advertising, television and movies, and a hundred other sources. You may even find yourself in situations where it could be easy to yield to sexual temptation.

One of the best ways of fighting back is learning to like yourself. If you feel good about you, you'll have the confidence to take a stand—even if you're the only one! Just remember who you are and what your parents have taught you. There's real strength in knowing that God loves you and has a purpose for your life!

But if you feel inferior to others, it will be that much easier to let them press you into their mold. Don't do it! The rest of your life is ahead of you, and it's worth fighting for. I hope this helps, Jonathan. I'm sure you dad will have more to say on this subject.

You're a lucky guy to have parents who care about you so much! Take advantage of their wisdom and be encouraged by their love. God bless you!

Jonathan was amazed to learn the letter was signed by James Dobson, whom I met 12 years ago. In fact, my inspiration for the key talk came from Dr. Dobson. In his first book, *Dare to Discipline*, Dr. Dobson described his intention to give his daughter, Danae, a small gold key that would represent the key to her heart.

A Parent's Influence

My key talk with Jonathan was one of the most memorable and moving experiences I've ever had. It seemed our hearts were bonded together.

Young people are romantics. They have a real need to identify their personal self-worth. Wholesome, biblical thoughts instilled during their tender years open an avenue for parents to discuss sex with their children. The importance a parent places on the key talk will greatly influence the child's sexual behavior prior to marriage.

Key talks should happen when the child becomes interested in the opposite sex. That can be as young as 10 or as old as 17.

Obviously, the key ring is a powerful day-in-and-day-out reminder for the child. The more the child values his or her virginity, the more the key ring becomes a precious symbol of the commitment to God and the future spouse.

As I've shared the key ring idea with many families, I've learned that it's also a good idea for teens who have lost their virginity. Although they've jumped the gun, they can commit themselves to God to remain pure until their wedding day. Teens who have fallen short can become virgins again in the sight of God. Once they're forgiven, it is as though they had never sinned. The Lord tells us in Isaiah 43:25 that "I, even I, am He who blots out and cancels your transgressions, for My own sake, and I will not remember your sins."

As Jonathan and I left El Encanto's that night, a couple sitting at a nearby table stopped us. They couldn't help but notice something special had happened, they said.

Something special *had* happened, and it was between Jonathan, his wife-to-be, and the Lord.

🌸 🌸 🌸
Kimberli Durfield

When my mother told me she wanted to take me out to our favorite Mexican restaurant for my key talk, I was quite anxious.

Mom talked openly. She even drew pictures on napkins to explain several points. I especially remember her telling me that sex was not our idea, but God's, so it had to be good.

After the talk, Mom pulled out a beautiful silver key ring! She told me this was a sign of the commitment I was about to make. That afternoon, with Mom as my witness, I made a vow to the Lord to remain sexually pure. That ring has been a constant reminder—and gotten me through some tough times!

Anna Durfield

I was so excited about my key talk with Mom—it was like the first night out with just the ladies. I was surprised how I could speak out about my sexual feelings and not feel any guilt. Mom knew where I was coming from and how I was feeling sexually.

At my high school, classmates candidly tell everyone about their sexual experiences. They appear to be happy, but there's a void there. My key talk with Mom—and the promise I made to God—has given me the desire to stay right before the Lord.

I've had strong sexual feelings—I still do. I've had a boyfriend for nearly four years, and we've spent precious moments together. But because I've made a stand from Day One of our relationship not to have sex, I've been able to keep my covenant with God.

I'm 19 and still a virgin. I still have a way to go before I get married, but when I do, I hope God gives me a man strong enough to handle this very healthy lady!

Timothy Durfield

I remember anticipating the day I would make a long-term commitment to God. I felt I was doing something that would make God happy with me. God has always been someone I've wanted to please, and I know if I keep this covenant with Him and don't break it, God will smile upon me.

I've kept that commitment for three years now. God has blessed me in that I've only gone out with girls who have the same morals as I. I'm still tempted, but that ring on my finger reminds me of my covenant with God and the gift I'll someday give to my wife.

Parents wanting more information about "key talks" should read the Durfields' book, *Raising Them Chaste* (Bethany House), or purchase key rings sold in Bob Siemon Jewelers' display cases. Both items are available in most Christian bookstores.

PART FOUR

FOCUS ON DIFFICULT FAMILY PROBLEMS

19

When God Doesn't Make Sense

James C. Dobson, Ph.D.

*T*he 11th chapter of Hebrews bears relevance to believers who have gone through great sorrow and suffering. Described in that chapter are the men and women who persevered in hardship and danger for the sake of the Cross.

Some were tortured, imprisoned, flogged, stoned, sawed in two, and put to death by the sword. They were destitute, mistreated, persecuted, and inadequately clothed. They wandered in deserts, in mountains, in caves, and in holes in the ground.

It is most important to understand that "they died not receiving what they had been promised." In other words, they held onto their faith to the point of death, even though God had not explained what He was doing (Heb. 11:35-40).

Without detracting from the sacredness of that Scripture, I would like to submit for your inspiration my own modern-day "Heroes' Hall of Fame." Listed among these giants of the faith are two incredible human beings who must hold a special place in the great heart of God.

During my 14 years on the attending staff at Children's Hospital in Los Angeles, many of the kids I saw suffered from terminal illnesses. Others endured chronic disorders that disrupted and warped their childhoods.

Some of them were less than 10 years of age, and yet their faith in Jesus Christ was unshakable. They died with a testimony on their lips, witnessing to the goodness of God while their little bodies withered away. What a reception they must have received when they met Him who said, "Suffer the little children to come unto me . . ." (Mark 10:14, KJV).

Bells Were Ringing

In my first film series, "Focus on the Family," I shared a story about a five-year-old African-American boy who will never be forgotten by those who knew him. A nurse with whom I worked, Gracie Schaeffler, took care of this lad during the latter days of his life. He was dying of lung cancer, which is a terrifying disease in its final stages. The lungs fill with fluid, and the patient is unable to breathe. It is terribly claustrophobic, especially for a small child.

This little boy had a Christian mother who loved him and stayed by his side though the long ordeal. She cradled him on her lap and talked softly about the Lord. Instinctively, the woman was preparing her son for the final hours to come. Gracie told me that she entered his room one day as death approached, and she heard this lad talking about hearing bells.

"The bells are ringing, Mommie," he said. "I can hear them."

Gracie thought he was hallucinating because he was already slipping away. She left and returned a few minutes later and again heard him talking about hearing bells ringing.

The nurse said to his mother, "I'm sure you know your baby is hearing things that aren't there. He is hallucinating because of the sickness."

The mother pulled her son closer to her chest, smiled, and said, "No, Miss Schaeffler. He is not hallucinating. I told him when he was frightened—when he couldn't breathe—if he would listen carefully, he could hear the bells of heaven ringing for him. That is what he's been talking about all day."

That precious child died on his mother's lap later that evening, and he was still talking about the bells of heaven when the angels came to take him. What a brave little trooper he was! His courage was not reported in the newspapers the next day. Neither Tom Brokaw nor Dan Rather told his story on the evening news. Yet he and his mother belong forever in our "Heroes' Hall of Fame."

My next candidate for faithful immortality is a man I never met, although he touched my life while he was losing his. I learned about him from a television docudrama that I saw many years ago. The producer had obtained permission from a cancer specialist to place cameras in his clinic.

Then with approval from three patients, two men and a woman, he captured on film the moment each of them learned they were afflicted with a malignancy in its later stages. Their initial shock, disbelief, fear, and anger were recorded in graphic detail.

Afterward, the documentary team followed these three families through the treatment process with its ups and downs, hopes and disappointments, pain and terror. I sat riveted as the drama of life and death unfolded on the screen. Eventually, all three patients died, and the program ended without comment or editorial.

There was so much that should have been said. What struck me were the different ways these people dealt with their frightening circumstances. The two who apparently had no faith reacted with anger and bitterness. They not only fought their disease, but seemed to be at war with everyone else. Their personal relationships, and even their marriages, were shaken—especially as the end drew near.

I'm not being critical, mind you. Most of us would respond in much the same manner if faced with imminent death. But that's what made the third individual so inspiring to me.

He was a humble, black pastor of a small inner-city Baptist church. He was in his late 60s and had been a minister throughout his adult life. His love for the Lord was so profound that it was reflected in everything he said.

When he and his wife were told he had only a few months to live, they revealed no panic. They quietly asked the doctor what it all meant. When he had explained the treatment program and what they could anticipate, they politely thanked him for his concern and departed. The cameras followed this little couple to their old car and eavesdropped as they bowed their heads and recommitted themselves to the Lord.

In the months that followed, the pastor never lost his poise. Nor was he glib about his illness. He was not in denial, he simply had come to terms with the cancer and its probable outcome. He knew the Lord was in control, and he refused to be shaken in his faith.

The cameras were present on his final Sunday in his church. He preached the sermon that morning and talked openly about his impending death. To the best of my recollection, this is what he said:

"Some of you have asked me if I'm mad at God for this disease that has taken over my body. I'll tell you honestly that I have nothing but love in my heart for my Lord. He didn't do this to me. We live in a sinful world where sickness and death are the curse man has brought upon himself. And I'm going to a better place where there will be no more tears, no suffering, and no heartache. So don't feel bad for me.

"Besides," he continued, "our Lord suffered and died for our sins. Why should I not share in His suffering?" Then he began to sing, without accompaniment, in an old broken voice:

> Must Jesus bear the cross alone,
> And all the world go free?

No, there's a cross for everyone,
And there's a cross for me.
How happy are the saints above,
Who once went sorr'wing here;
But now they taste unmingled love,
And joy without a tear.
The consecrated cross I'll bear,
Till death shall set me free,
And then go home my crown to wear,
For there's a crown for me.

I wept as this gentle man sang of his love for Jesus. He sounded very weak, and his face was drawn from the ravages of the disease. But his comments were as powerful as any I've ever heard. His words that morning were his last from the pulpit, as far as I know. He slipped into eternity a few days later, where he met the Lord he had served for a lifetime. This unnamed pastor and his wife have a prominent place among my list of spiritual giants.

Pieces to Life's Puzzle

There are more heroes in my catalog than I could describe, but I will resist the inclination to name them. My concern at this point, however, is to help those who are not so well grounded in their beliefs. If everyone was gifted with the tenacity of a bulldog and the faith of Father Abraham, there would be no need for a discussion of this nature. But most of us are not spiritual superstars.

That's why these thoughts are addressed affectionately to individuals who have been wounded in spirit by experiences they could not understand. The pieces to life's puzzle simply have not fit together, leaving them confused, angry, and disillusioned.

Perhaps you are among those who have struggled to comprehend a particular heartache and God's reason for allowing it. A thousand unanswered questions have been recycling in your mind—most of them beginning with the word, "Why?"

You want desperately to trust the Father and believe in His grace and goodness. But deep inside, you're held captive by a sense of betrayal and abandonment. The Lord obviously permitted your difficulties to occur. Why didn't He prevent them—and why has He not attempted to explain or apologize for them? The inability to answer those fundamental questions has become a spiritual barrier a mile high, and you can't seem to find a way around or over it.

For some of my readers, your sorrow can be traced directly to the death of a precious son or daughter. Your pain from that loss has been so intense that you've wondered if you could even carry on. What a joy he (or she) was to your heart. He ran and jumped and giggled and hugged. You loved him far more than you valued your own life.

But then, there was that horrible morning at the pool, or the ominous medical report, or the accident on the bicycle. Now your beloved child is gone, and God's purpose in his death has remained a mystery.

For someone else, there will never be anything as painful as the rejection you were dealt by an ex-husband or wife. The day you discovered the infidelity, or when the divorce papers arrived at the door, or that unforgettable night of violence—those were indescribable moments of heartache.

In some ways, it would have been easier to have buried the spouse than to see him or her in the arms of another. How could that person to whom you gave everything be so cruel? Many tears were shed as God was begged to intervene. When the marriage continued to fail, disillusionment and bitterness rolled over you like a tidal wave. You've said you would never trust anyone again—not even the Almighty.

I'm thinking also of widows and widowers trying to survive on their own. If you're one of them, you know what very few of your friends fully comprehend. They want you to get over this loss and return to the business of living. But you just can't do it. For so many years, your marriage was the centerpiece of your existence. Two separate human beings truly became "one flesh" as God intended. It was such a sweet love affair that it could have gone on forever.

In fact, when you were young, you honestly thought it would. But suddenly, it was over. And now, for the first time in many years, you're truly alone. Is this what it all comes down to?

To those whom I have been describing—those who have struggled to understand God's providence—I bring hope to you today. No, I can't provide tidy little solutions to all of life's annoying inconsistencies. That will not occur until we see the Lord face to face.

But His heart is especially tender toward the downtrodden and the defeated. He knows your name, and He has seen every tear you have shed. He was there on each occasion when life took a wrong turn. And what appears to be divine disinterest or cruelty is a misunderstanding at best and a satanic lie at worst.

How do I know this to be true? Because the Scriptures emphatically tell us so. For starters, David wrote, "The Lord is close to the brokenhearted and saves those who are crushed in spirit" (Psalm 34:18). Isn't that a beautiful verse?

How encouraging to know that the very presence of the King— the Creator of all heaven and earth—hovers near those who are wounded and discouraged. If you could fully comprehend how deeply you are loved, you would never feel alone again.

David returned to that thought in Psalm 103:11: "For as high as the heavens are above the earth, so great is his love for those who fear him. . . ."

Another favorite passage is Romans 8:26, in which we're told that the Holy Spirit actually prays for you and me with such passion that human language is inadequate to describe it. That verse says, "In the same way, the Spirit helps us in our weakness. We do not know what we ought to pray, but the Spirit himself intercedes for us with groans that words cannot express."

What comfort we should draw from that understanding! He is calling your name to the Father today, pleading your case and describing your need. How wrong it is, therefore, to place the blame for your troubles on the best friend mankind ever had! Regardless of other conclusions you draw, please believe this: He is not the source of your pain!

Explanations

If you were sitting before me at this moment, you might be inclined to ask, "Then how do you explain the tragedies and hardships that have come into my life? Why did God do this to me?" My reply is not profound, but I know it is right! God rarely chooses to answer those questions in this life!

That's what I've been trying to say. He will not parade His plans and purposes for our approval. We must never forget that He is God. As such, He wants us to believe and trust in Him despite the things we don't understand. It's that straightforward.

Jehovah never did answer Job's intelligent inquiries, and He will not respond to all of yours. Every person who ever lived, I submit, has had to deal with seeming contradictions and enigmas. You will not be the exception.

If that explanation is unsatisfactory, and you can't accept it, then you are destined to go through life with a weak, ineffectual faith—or no faith at all. You'll just have to construct your castles on some other foundation. That will be your greatest challenge, however—because there is no other foundation. It is written, "Except the Lord build a house, they labor in vain which build it" (Psalm 127:1, KJV).

My strongest advice is that each of us acknowledge before the crisis occurs, if possible, that our trust in Him must be independent of our understanding. There's nothing wrong with trying to understand, but we must not lean on our ability to comprehend!

Sooner or later our intellect will pose questions we cannot possibly answer. At that point, we would be wise to remember His words, "As the heavens are higher than the earth, so are my ways higher than you ways and my thoughts than your thoughts" (Is. 55:9). And our reply should be "Not my will, but thine be done" (Luke 22:42, KJV).

For those who are hurting and discouraged, I think it would be comforting to look forward to the time when the present trials will be a distant memory. A day of celebration is coming like nothing that has ever occurred in the history of mankind.

The Guest of Honor on that morning will be One wearing a seamless robe, with eyes like flames of fire and feet like fine brass. As we bow humbly before Him, a Great Voice will thunder from the heavens, saying:

> Behold, the tabernacle of God is with men, and He will dwell with them, and they shall be His people, and God Himself will be with them and be their God. And God will wipe away every tear from their eyes; there shall be no more death, nor sorrow, nor crying, and there shall be nor more pain, for the former things have passed away (Rev. 21:3-4, KJV).

And, again, the Mighty Voice will echo through the corridors of time:

> They shall neither hunger anymore nor thirst anymore; the sun shall not strike them, nor any heat; for the Lamb who is in the midst of the throne will shepherd them and lead them to living fountains of waters. And God will wipe every tear from their eyes (Rev. 7:16-17, KJV).

This is the hope of the ages that burns within my breast. It is the ultimate answer to those who suffer and struggle today. It is the only solace for those who have said goodbye to a loved one. Though the pain is indescribable now, we must never forget that our separation is temporary. We will be reunited forever on that glad resurrection morning. As the Scripture promises, our tears will be banished forever!

My father and mother will also be in the crowd on that day, standing expectantly beside my little grandmother, who prayed for me before I was born. They will be straining to catch a glimpse of our arrival, just like they did so many Christmas seasons when we flew into the Kansas City airport. Dad will have so much to tell me, he will be bursting with excitement. He'll want to take me to some distant planet he's discovered.

Your loved ones who died in Christ will also be in that great throng, singing and shouting the praises of the Redeemer. What a celebration it will be!

This is the reward for the faithful—for those who overcome their sense of betrayal in tough times and persevere to the end. This is the crown of righteousness prepared for those who have fought a good fight, finished the course, and kept the faith (2 Tim. 4:7).

Final Thoughts

Throughout our remaining days in this life, therefore, let me urge you not to be discouraged by temporal cares. Accept the circumstances as they are presented to you. Expect periods of hardship to occur, and don't be dismayed when they arrive. "Lean into the pain" when your time to suffer comes around, knowing that God will use the difficult for His purposes—and indeed, for your own good. The Lord is very near, and He has promised that your temptation will not be greater than you can bear (1 Cor. 10:13).

I'll leave you with these wonderful verses from the 34th Psalm:

> The righteous cry out, and the Lord hears them; he delivers them from all their troubles. The Lord is close to the brokenhearted and saves those who are crushed in spirit. A righteous man may have many troubles, but the Lord delivers him from them all"(v. 17-19).

This chapter is adapted from When God Doesn't Make Sense by Dr. James Dobson, © 1993 James Dobson, Inc. Used by permission of Tyndale House Publishers, Inc.

20

When Mom Is Really Sick

Cynthia Culp Allen

My doctor left the room to determine my diagnosis. While he was out, I sat on the hard table, clutching the flimsy paper robe as though it was my last piece of dignity. For months, I'd endured test after test, trying to uncover the reason for my miserable health. I hoped this time to get an answer.

Dr. Thomson breezed back into the room.

"Lupus," he pronounced matter-of-factly in a voice as cold as the examining room. "I'm giving you a tentative diagnosis of lupus erythematosus."

My heart fell. Lupus is an incurable disease that causes the body's immune system to attack its own tissue.

I knew it was something horrible, I thought. I had been desperately ill for months. The disease affected my central nervous system, and

I was hit with dizziness, headaches, ringing ears, memory loss, and confusion. Finally, I was unable to continue my normal routine and was forced to stay in bed. My grandmother moved in and took over my role of homemaker and mom. The only responsibility I could continue was reading the daily Bible story to my children, something I could do from my bed.

Helping Out

Even with the correct diagnosis, five years passed before I could return to my normal schedule. And even then it was with limitations. But out of my own illness, God gave me a special empathy for the infirm and a rewarding new ministry—caring for other sick moms.

A mother is not only the heart of the home but its hub. When she's ill, life around the house ceases to roll smoothly. But family and friends can help an incapacitated mother in numerous ways. Here are 16 suggestions to "bear one another's burdens" from one who's been there:

• **Pray for your friend and her family.** Pray for healing, yes, but also pray that God will be glorified in the situation. Our Great Physician knows her illness and the outcome of it. As I studied the Old Testament accounts of how God worked in the lives of the ancient believers, I saw the mercy, faithfulness, and power that God revealed through mighty miracles. As I realized that He never changes, I was reassured that the same great, powerful God would be with me in my illness.

• **Avoid platitudes.** "I understand just what you're going through" isn't encouraging when your sick friend knows you don't even suffer from monthly cramps.

"We'll be praying for you" is more reassuring. But it's even better to pray with her right at the time. Nothing will comfort your friend more than being able to hold your hand and pray together about her burden.

• **Express heartfelt concern.** What should you say? "I'm sorry you're going through this" is a genuine statement. "Can I do something?" is always welcome.

Don't say, "Call if you need something." (She won't.) Instead, call to ask how you can help.

- **Provide meals.** Taking in dinner is one of the best assistances. However, check to see if the sick mom or anyone in the family is on a special diet. A strict diet was crucial to my recovery, so it was a treat when I could eat prepared meals with the others.

- **When you visit, be interested in the person's illness.** (Or at least act as though you are!) If your sick friend wants to talk about it, be a good listener. While a person is engulfed in a serious illness, her mind doesn't have room to squeeze in much else. She needs to express her fears, anxieties, and hope—just as Job did.

- **Avoid dramatic monologues of all the exciting things you and your family are doing.** Hearing about your latest vacation—from start to finish—can be discouraging to a mom who's sick in bed. Our society emphasizes activity and productivity. I lay in bed for a year (and my life was "on hold" for several more), so I felt guilty that I couldn't be the fun, capable mom I wanted to be.

Encourage your sick friend with these words: "Just rest and concentrate on getting well. The world will take care of itself while you recuperate."

- **When you phone or visit, keep it "short and sweet."** Most sick people don't have the strength for long visits or phone conversations, but frequent brief communications, even notes, show you are still thinking of her. The isolation of an illness can be overwhelming, so do visit. Just remember to phone before you drop by.

- **Take along personal gifts.** Do you know something your friend would especially like? Perhaps a certain perfume or a bouquet of flowers? What are her reading or music preferences? Gifts chosen with her in mind will make her smile

A friend from church provided me with tapes of the services. I was unable to attend worship for months, so this thoughtful gift kept me connected during my convalescence. Listening to the routine announcements, songs of praise, and the pastor's sermon brightened my gloomy week.

- **When you visit, leave your own children behind.** Perhaps you could trade baby-sitting with another friend and alternate your visits.

Once, two mothers dropped by to "cheer me up." They brought a craft project to work on—and five children. It was lunch time, and my three children were being fed. Of course, their group was hungry, too.

We sat the eight children with their bowls of soup (the only food I had for a crowd) on a blanket, picnic style. As they were eating, the cat jumped onto the blanket. One of the moms kicked at the cat, missed, and sent a bowl of soup flying like a Scud missile across my living room. Vegetable soup splattered all over my walls and carpet. The bowl hit the sliding glass door and exploded. The visit was ruined.

- **Make your friends laugh.** Deliver funny cards, books, or videos to your housebound friend. During my illness, I discovered that when I was laughing, I didn't notice the pain as much.

- **Clean your friend's house.** The old bromide "Cleanliness is next to godliness" went out the kitchen window when I became sick. Having lower standards depressed me, and I'm sure my family as well.

Clean for your friend, but don't comment on the mess—to her or anyone else. It's embarrassing when the friend who scrubs your refrigerator spreads a vicious rumor that you're growing your own penicillin to save money.

- **Watch your friend's children.** As dear as children are, they are difficult for even a *healthy* mom to keep up with. Children continue their usual challenges while mom is sick. Sometimes, their antics even escalate.

When mom is sick, life often dwindles to the necessities. Your friend's children will enjoy being included in fun activities and projects.

- **Be your friend's chauffeur.** At my sickest point, I was in and out of the hospital for tests and consultations. One friend, Norma, agreed to be "on call" for the 20-mile drive, and she was a tremendous help when I developed life-threatening complications.

Remember that life continues for the sick mom's family. They still have to be driven to Little League games, Bible clubs, and after-school lessons. Groceries must still be bought and errands run. Your help will be a great encouragement to the whole family.

• **Help financially.** With a long-term illness, bills pile up even with good insurance. This is one way the church can help, but any kind of assistance will be appreciated. Even a bag of groceries shows you care.

• **Alleviate holiday stress.** The autumn I was in bed, my mother came up with imaginative costumes so my children could attend a Harvest Festival.

Christmas offers an even greater challenge. A sick mom will appreciate your helping with the decorations and baking. You can also take her shopping and even select and wrap the gifts. Her children may also need you to take them to parties and programs. It's important that they don't miss out on the joy of the season.

• **Continue your support.** Many friends give aid at the onset of a disease but forget as time goes on. The sick person is left alone to cope with prolonged disability. If you think you're tired of your friend's lengthy illness, imagine how she feels.

In closing, don't be overwhelmed by this "to do" list. Choose one thing you can do without jeopardizing your own family. If each friend helps in some way, it won't be a burden on any one person.

So, when a sick mom calls and says, "I was just at the doctor's, and he says I have . . . ," you can answer with, "Don't worry about a thing. I'll be right over. I know just what to do."

Cynthia Allen lives in La Habra, California.

21

Stepfamilies: Growing into Love

Lonni Collins Pratt

W hen David and I walked down the aisle five years ago, it was the second time for both of us. Our first marriages had ended in divorce.

Between us, we brought five teenagers to our new family. I had two daughters, Shelly and Andrea. Although David's three children, Mike, Scott, and Michelle, lived with their mother, they spent weekends and holiday periods with us.

The first Christmas was a disaster. The boys didn't like their gifts. The girls bickered, and one wanted all her presents returned. My Shelly called Michelle a brat. We ended the evening with most of us in tears.

When the next holiday season arrived, I wasn't expecting much. As if to downplay the event, I prepared tacos and chili for Christmas Eve dinner. When we all sat down at the table, David led the family in prayer.

"Thank You, Lord, for our children," he began, "and thank You for this chance to celebrate Your love as a family. Help us to understand and be patient with each other. Thank You for the gift of life in Jesus. Happy birthday."

Silence followed, then Shelly poked Scott. "At least it was short," she chortled. "You should hear him pray when you guys aren't here. He prays for everything but the food."

It dawned on me that David's children had never heard their father pray. He had committed his life to Christ *after* the divorce.

David's short prayer broke the ice. Before tearing into gifts, we strung cranberries and made popcorn balls. Then came the presents. After a few minutes, the sound of ripping paper ceased. Scott had found the bottle of bubbles. The other kids quickly unwrapped their similarly shaped gifts. The bubbles had been David's idea.

Within minutes, our nearly grown children, all five of them, were chasing each other around the house, blowing bubbles and laughing like little kids.

I wish I could have videotaped the commotion. So many things that other families take for granted were surprise gifts for us. But that's to be expected when you're trying to blend two families.

Starting Over

One out of every three Americans is either a stepparent, a stepchild, a stepsibling, or some other member of a stepfamily. According to the Census Bureau, the number of children living with their biological mother and a stepfather increased 13 percent to six million between 1980 and 1985 (the latest figures available), and the number living with a stepmother and a biological father increased 2 percent to 740,000. Undoubtedly, these numbers are even higher today.

When David and I decided to get married, we knew that successfully blending our families wasn't going to happen overnight, given the advanced ages of our children. My first inkling of trouble occurred when two of his children, Scott and Michelle, didn't attend our wedding. Then David's ex-wife demanded that he not tell me anything she had told him about their children. He replied that he couldn't agree to her request since I was his wife. Most of their telephone conversations ended with angry, raised voices.

After David and I returned from our honeymoon, my daughter Shelly, then 14, and I had our own skirmishes. Our battlegrounds were the usual for mothers and daughters: dating, school, curfews. Against my wishes, she went to live with her father.

Suddenly, Andrea was the only child in the house. But she challenged David's authority from the start—even in unimportant matters. If he asked her to get her books off the kitchen table, she would bark, "You aren't my father!"

After just two weeks, we knew the task of blending our families would be even more difficult than we had imagined. Through trial and error, through tears and hugs, here are some things we've learned over the past five years:

• **Make your marriage a priority.** David and I did not rush into marriage. As Christians, we were both very anxious for more of God's presence this time around. Why? We knew that the odds of second marriages lasting are even lower than first marriages.

Before our wedding, we sat down with each of the children and explained to them that, next to God, our marriage would be given top priority. Of course, we assured them that we would love them as always, but we were adding the new responsibility of loving a spouse, too.

But during our post-wedding upheaval, I lost sight of why David and I were together. Instead, I saw only problems. Deep inside, I blamed David because Shelly moved out. I worried if his children would ever accept me. Silence and anger crept into our relationship.

One evening, David and I had a heart-to-heart talk. "I don't know what's ahead, Honey," he began, "but I don't want anything to come between us. I'd certainly be angry if one of my children had left. I might even blame you."

After we talked about our feelings, we recommitted ourselves to each other and our marriage, and then we went to our knees. "Lord, help us to love," prayed David. "We have made this commitment. Let the children see Your love in our marriage. We are determined to serve You together. Help us be patient and tender."

• **Find a church that is supportive and understanding.** Each Sunday morning, David and I attend a class for divorced singles and remarried couples. I listen to others talk about their teenage children and the problems of raising them in a stepfamily. It is such a comfort to know that other parents and children struggle with the same problems. We aren't bad parents, and our children aren't rotten.

While we heard from other couples who had to deal with condemnation from church members for divorce and remarriage, our church restored us in loving forgiveness. No wonder statistics indicate that most single adults leave the church after a divorce because they feel judged and condemned.

The old African proverb is true: "It takes a village to raise a child." It is never more true than in the case of stepfamilies. The church needs to be that village.

• **The stepparent can rely on the biological parent's authority until a relationship is established.** When a stepparent walks in the door and demands immediate authority, he or she is asking for trouble. Experts say it takes at least two years before a child even *begins* to accept the stepparent. We found this to be true.

Once, when I was gone for a weekend, David and Andrea got into another battle of wills. She wanted to go to a party that would not be supervised by adults. None of David's reasons for saying no were acceptable to her.

Finally, he called me and asked what I thought. "Tell her *I* said no," I said.

He did.

I could hear Andrea snap in the distinctive tone of angry female teenagers: "Well, why not?" she wailed.

I replied to David, "Tell her because I'm her mother, and you are the one I have trusted to care for her—that's why!"

End of discussion.

After that incident, David started saying, "Your mother would like you to clean your room." "Do you think Mom would like you to watch this movie?" "Did your mother tell you it was okay to go?"

He relied upon my established authority, and I did the same with his children. We have been slowly doing this less and less as our stepchildren learn to trust us.

• **Seize every opportunity to establish trust.** Several years back, a younger Andrea trotted past me with a model car in her hand. She found David in the living room reading the paper.

"I glued the doors shut," she groaned. "Can you fix it?" She flopped down beside him, and soon their heads were bent over the model. From across the room, I silently thanked God for the tiny gift of trust my daughter offered her stepfather.

A tiny step? Sure. But we know that blended families move toward unity one tiny step at a time, and each movement is a miracle. Individuals who think they can go into a household and snap everyone into line will soon completely dismantle whatever is left of the family.

God has given us unique opportunities to prove our trustworthiness. But we have to be looking for them with one wet finger lifted to the air, waiting for the breeze of divine opportunity.

• **Realize emergencies will occur.** Shortly after she moved back with us, Shelly's child development class was given the assignment of parenting an egg. She had to keep the egg "baby" with her at all times for a week. She was allowed two hours away from it each day, but only if she had a dependable egg-sitter. If the egg-baby broke, she flunked.

Shelly was scheduled for outpatient tests at the hospital. She nervously left her egg-baby with David in the waiting room. A friend of my husband's, an orthopedic surgeon, saw him waiting and went over to say hello.

David stood up to shake his hand. The egg fell off the chair and cracked.

When Shelly returned to the waiting area, a nurse told her the egg was in the emergency room. She found her stepfather tenderly holding her egg-baby, as his surgeon friend put a tiny cast on it. The doctor said it was a hairline fracture, and the "baby chicken would live."

Shelly laughed as she talked about it at dinner that night. She grinned at David and said, "If you baby-sit your grandchildren, I'll just have to put crash helmets on them."

David nudged my leg under the table. We both heard it—*"your* grandchildren."

• **Relationships grow with time.** Much of what binds a family is found in the history of living and loving together. As a stepfamily, we must build our history, bit by bit, from the ground up.

In small ways, we tried to make our support concrete for our young-adult children. We made every effort to be a sounding board for summer camp, college, classes, special trips, and summer employ-ment. While not investing less time in our marriage, we made it one of our top priorities to encourage and love our five children.

We made a determined effort to attend band and choir concerts, plays, baseball games, graduations, and award ceremonies. We even dropped by and bought chocolate eclairs when my daughter landed her first "real" job at a local donut shop.

Gradually, we noticed our family coming together. It will never look like a traditional family, but we've accepted that.

Once, we came home to find a son sprawled on the sofa watching basketball and eating popcorn. He must have felt "at home" to do that. Believe it or not, it was a milestone when the boys stopped using the doorbell. Another time, Scott and I got into a debate about the ethics of nuclear weapons. Mike, Shelly, and Andrea argue like . . . well, brothers and sisters. Andrea and Michelle compare notes on how unreasonable mothers can be.

The other day, Shelly called Scott her "big brother." He looked confused for a moment—I waited for him to deny the title. He didn't. He grinned and told her she's a pest.

In more ways than one, that was perfectly fine with me.

Lonni Collins Pratt and her family live in Lapeer, Michigan.

22

Picking Up
the Pieces

Mike Yorkey

One afternoon, while three-year-old Emilie was sitting on her potty chair, she rolled a piece of toilet tissue into a cigarette-shaped form.

"Whatcha doing?" asked her grandmother, Nellie Morse, as Emilie worked her little fingers around the tissue.

"I'm rolling a joint," she replied.

"Who taught you how to do that?"

"My mamma and her friend. They taught me."

That's when Nellie knew she had to confront her 24-year-old daughter, Marilyn, who had traded life as a hard-working single mom for the fast lane of bikes, booze, and drugs. For months, Marilyn had been hanging out with a motorcycle gang and a succession of long-haired boyfriends.

"I know you're fooling with drugs," Nellie told her daughter when

177

she came to pick up Emilie.

"Who told you that?" Marilyn asked.

"The baby."

"Oh, Mother, she just made that up."

"Babies don't lie. She wouldn't know *how* to make up something like that. If you're not going to straighten up and raise her right, why don't you just leave her with us?"

Marilyn slowly nodded. Within a few weeks, she appeared before a judge to sign the necessary adoption papers, granting her parents custody of young Emilie.

Those legal proceedings happened nearly nine years ago, and today, Nellie, and her husband, Grant, count themselves among an increasing number of grandparents who are being recycled—as parents to their children's children. According to 1990 Census Bureau figures, nearly 1 million grandparents are raising grandchildren by themselves, and another 1.5 million grandparents have opened their homes to grandchildren and a son or daughter, as well. Thus, approximately 5 percent of American families represent a grandparent raising a grandchild.

"I don't think many of us understand how serious the problem is," says Irene Endicott, a grandmother of 12 and author of *Grandparenting Redefined.* "At a time when older people are supposed to be enjoying the fruits of their labors and thinking about retirement, they are chasing four- and five-year-olds around and using up all their retirement funds in the process."

Grandparents raising grandchildren is not a new phenomenon. For centuries, grandparents have stepped in and raised children orphaned through disease or war. Closer to our era, President Bill Clinton lived as a young boy with grandparents while his mother studied nursing in Louisiana. But in the last decade, the number of grandchildren living with grandparents has shot up 37 percent, a rise paralleling the swelling numbers of single parents and out-of-wedlock births.

Why the sudden increase?

Blame it on the four D's: drugs, divorce, desertion, and death of a parent. "Substance abuse is by far the number-one cause of grandparents' legal custody of their grandchildren," says Mrs. Endicott, "Young single mothers, already addicted or unable to cope with their situations, turn to drugs for a way out. It's the children—malnourished and emotionally neglected—who suffer the most.

"Divorce also ranks right up there," adds Mrs. Endicott. "The doorbell rings at 10:15 at night, you open the door, and it's your daughter. She's got your grandbaby in her arms and she's crying. 'He's gone, Mom. He left me,' she says. 'Can we stay with you?' "

Few parents can refuse such a request, not when flesh and blood are involved. Nor can grandparents deny Scripture. In 1 Timothy 5:8, Paul writes, "If anyone does not provide for his relatives, and especially for his immediate family, he has denied the faith and is worse than an unbeliever."

Special Challenges

For Norman and Marge McGarry, there was never any question they would take in two-year-old Paula when her mother—a single parent—died of a brain aneurysm at 27. "It was easy to get custody," said Marge. "The father had no contact with Paula, so he did not contest the adoption."

Parenting a second time has been more difficult for the McGarrys, who are in their mid-50s. "We raised five children, and we were certainly more active with them, playing ball in the back yard and going on snowmobile trips in the winter. These days, it's all we can do to keep up with Paula. We're just not as active as we once were."

Grandparents in their 50s and 60s know they don't have as much stamina for middle-of-the-night bottle feedings or keeping tabs on energetic youngsters. Others are at an age where their bodies are starting to break down. Fifty-six-year-old Nellie Morse, for instance, has survived two bouts of cancer. Five years ago, doctors informed her she had a year to live, but she was determined to beat that prognosis. "I'm still alive," says Nellie, "but I'm scared to death that I won't live to raise Emilie."

Taking in grandchildren usually resigns grandparents to a penny-pinching retirement. For many, their high-income earning years are a memory, and they are living on a modest pension or fixed income. Many must dip into savings or sell their homes—nest eggs they expected to tap later in life.

"It's a real financial burden," agrees Doris Hawkins, a Detroit-area grandmother. Her daughter, Nancy, became a single parent shortly after high school graduation. Doris and her husband, Tom, offered to care for Robby while Nancy worked at Michigan Bell. Then her daughter was transferred to another town, but she couldn't afford day care on her meager salary, so Doris and Tom offered to keep Robby.

"We all thought this was going to be a temporary arrangement, but then Nancy had another baby out-of-wedlock, and we had to look after him," said Doris. "Her life was really messed up."

Caring for two children also messed up the Hawkinses' retirement plans. "Tom and I were looking forward to moving to the Carolinas when we retire, but that is now out of the question. We'd already raised a family, but what were we going to do? Those little kids are kin."

Both children are attending a Christian elementary school, and the Hawkinses are determined to learn from the mistakes they made the first time around. "When our kids were teenagers, we got out of the habit of going to church," said Doris. "I feel a lot of responsibility for that, because we got lazy when Nancy needed it most. This is our second chance to make things right."

Custody Battles

When Pete and Peggy Jackson married 25 years ago, they wanted to have children right away—with the idea that they would still be on the sunny side of 40 when their children left home.

Peggy became a mother at 20, when Sandra was born. A brother, Andrew, arrived two years later. Sandra grew up in the church and loved studying the Bible. She had an independent streak, however, and upon high school graduation, Sandra announced her intention to marry a troubled young man named Jack. "We didn't approve of the marriage, but Sandra was 18, so there was nothing we could do about it," said Peggy. "They were both young and immature, and he had a strong history of alcohol and drug abuse. He once lost his driver's license for several months because he was caught driving under the influence."

They began to have problems early in their marriage, and Sandra soon joined her husband's alcoholic binges. Drugs then entered the picture. Despite their rocky relationship, Sandra gave birth to two daughters, Heather and Nicole. In 1990, when the children were two and one, a drug-addled Sandra attempted suicide and landed in a psychiatric ward for 30 days. Health and Rehabilitative Services (HRS) authorities were going to put the two infants in foster care until the Jacksons took temporary custody. While they disapproved of their daughter's lifestyle, Pete and Peggy felt the children should not have to pay for the sins of the parents.

After Sandra left the mental hospital, she and Jack took the kids and moved to a nearby town. Meanwhile, the downward spiral continued. To earn enough money to support her drug habit, Sandra became an exotic dancer in a topless bar, but she knew that dancing by night and doing drugs by day was no way to raise a family.

"That's when I got a call from my daughter, asking if I would take the kids," said Peggy. "When those precious girls came to live with us, they were emotionally and physically exhausted. It was a real adjustment for them to settle into a stable home life. For the first year, they couldn't sleep. All they did was whine and cry. I could only hold those little girls and rock them. I lost 25 pounds just trying to get through it."

Then Sandra and Jack asked if they could move in with the Jacksons until they got their lives in order. "I said okay, but only for a short time," said Peggy. "I really wanted them to work out their marriage and get the children back. But six weeks later, Jack beat up Sandra in our home, and then he tried to rape her in front of the 18-month-old. The child still remembers that incident to this day.

Sandra left Jack and moved to another town, where she moved in with a boyfriend and started nude dancing again."

At this point, the Jacksons began adoption proceedings, but their daughter hired an attorney to fight them. Parents and daughter are now estranged. Meanwhile, HRS authorities are allowing the girls to stay with their grandparents.

Nellie Morse's legal battles are behind her. Today, she can concentrate on raising Emilie, who is a happy 12-year-old. But she has not seen her mom ever since she left the courtroom nine years ago. "Marilyn knows our phone number and where we live," Nellie says, "but I have no idea how to get in touch with her. She's only called a few times, usually at Christmas."

Once, when Nellie and much-younger Emilie went to the local mall, a bearded biker dressed in leather walked past. "She started shaking," recalled Nellie, "and she clung to me, saying, 'Granny, you won't make me go, will you?'

"I said, 'No, Baby, you won't ever have to go. You can live here as long as you want.' "

Pete and Peggy Jackson feel the same way about the two grandchildren they are raising. "Pete and I have suffered, but not like the children have," said Peggy. "We were looking forward to wherever the Lord wanted us to go, never thinking we would have to raise a family again.

"But God has taught us the valuable lesson that we can serve Him through these kids, and we're determined to do exactly that."

Emilie is a pseudonym, as are most of the names in this story.

23

Yes, There's Help for Hyperactive Children

Sandra Doran

I was washing my kitchen floor one morning when the call came from the nursery school. My son's young teacher was elusive, groping for words. Something was different about Eric. He seemed to have a hard time fitting into a structure and abiding by rules. Eric wasn't "bad," she assured me, but had I had his hearing checked? Could there be some trouble with his ability to process what others were saying?

I let the dirty water drip from the end of the mop while my mind struggled to define what she was saying. My tried-and-true parenting methods just hadn't worked, and I felt shame because I couldn't control my "unruly" child.

Seeking Answers

It would be a year before my husband and I would fully understand why Eric was the way he was. We began by visiting a clinical psychologist, who conducted a developmental history of Eric and observed our family in action. His diagnosis was clear: Our son was suffering from Attention-Deficit Hyperactive Disorder (ADHD).

Exactly what is this condition that characterizes 5 percent of school-age children today? Psychologist Mark Gang, Ph.D., of Fairfield, Connecticut, specializes in assessing and treating children with learning, behavioral, and adjustment difficulties. He lists five core symptoms of attention-deficit disorder.

• *Poor sustained attention.* These children get bored 50 percent faster than the average child. Thus, it is difficult for them to concentrate for long periods of time.

• *Impulsive, with poor delay of gratification.* In other words, they don't think; they just act. They often interrupt, find themselves in dangerous situations, and don't follow directions. In short, they do what seizes them at the moment without thinking through the consequences.

• *Behavior often characterized by hyperactivity.* These children move in quick, abrupt, and often disruptive bursts. It is interesting to note that although this term is commonly used to characterize the disorder, it is only *one* of five core symptoms and is present in 70 percent of the children—*not* 100 percent. Thus, it is possible to have a child who has attention-deficit disorder *without* hyperactivity.

• *Diminished rule-governing behavior.* They have difficulty following through with instructions, becoming easily focused on something else. Their tendency to be consumed by the moment interferes with the completion of the task.

• *Great variability of performance.* Just when you think you have these children figured out, they display an opposite tendency. Such children are commonly labeled as lazy in the classroom when the teacher discovers they can make A's one day but slide back into D's and F's the next. These children are consistently inconsistent.

Where to Start

If you suspect your child may be attention-deficit/hyperactive, begin by discussing this concern with a pediatrician, who can rule out any medical conditions that create similar behavioral patterns. For example, lead poisoning—which at times has symptoms very much like those displayed by the ADHD child—can be identified by a simple blood test.

Once other medical conditions have been eliminated, it is imperative to find a psychologist *whose specialty includes ADHD*. If the professional has a limited understanding of the disorder, you may find you and your family sidetracked down a frustrating path. Our own search for answers led us to spend hundreds of dollars and countless hours with a therapist who simply watched Eric "play" and formed conclusions unrelated to our reality.

For me, the process toward understanding began the day I spotted a flyer attached to the post office door. "Hyperactive? Inattentive? Impulsive?" the paper read. "Now there's support for parents of children with attention-deficit disorders."

The nonprofit organization Children and Adults with Attention-Deficit Disorders (CHADD) was begun by a group of parents who realized the tremendous need for support among families with the attention-deficit problem. Through monthly meetings, a newsletter, and networking, CHADD provides a system of caring for parents struggling to cope with ADHD children.

While you're learning more about this challenge, Dr. Gang suggests seven important things you can do to keep your family on track.

- *Become educated.* Find out as much as you can about ADHD. Accept the fact that it is a handicap and that you need to modify your environment. Don't expect your child to behave like others.

Anytime we must adjust our strong expectations, we face a real loss. Psychologists call it "the loss of a dream." Before you can begin to deal with your child's problem, it's important to face your own loss squarely. Realize it will not go away, but rather will present a tremendous challenge. All of this is part of the healthy grieving process.

• *Set up special environmental conditions.* What ADHD children need most is structure and consistency. They do best when they know exactly what is expected of them, and when they can function within a comfortable and predictable routine.

• *Understand what your priorities are.* Take a realistic look at your family. Don't try to accomplish more than is necessary.

• *Focus on the strengths of your child.* So often we spend the day haranguing the ADHD child for everything he does wrong. It's important to break this cycle and build his self-esteem. Each day provide opportunities for this child to do something he is good at.

• *Learn when to battle.* If we let them, a thousand minor annoyances will provide ample opportunity each day to drain our energy reserves. Save that energy for the really important issues.

• *Buffer your child from negative feedback.* Whenever possible, don't put your child in a position where it will be difficult for him to fit in. His social skills are often weak; he may not catch the nuances of social expectations among the neighborhood gang. There are days when you just have to put your child in the car and go to the library, the zoo, or the park.

• *Attend to yourself and your marriage.* Parenting the ADHD child is an overwhelming task. The statistics on marriages that don't handle the pressure are frightening. However, you *can* keep your marriage intact while struggling with a very demanding child.

Make a real effort to work as a team, sharing in the responsibility. It's important not to place blame for your child's condition, but rather to support each other as you attempt to reestablish harmony in the family.

Be sure to take time off together. You need it more than any average couple! Make time for yourselves as individuals, too. You may find that taking turns in giving care so the other parent can take even a simple walk will provide enormous relief.

A Knock on the Door

It has been several years since my husband and I discovered our son is ADHD. We have since learned that for each challenge God places in our lives, He provides blessings, too. Our son's boundless energy and endless questions are not all bad. While some days can be tempestuous and challenging, through it all we are raising a child whose heart goes out to the underdog, who begs us to stop and pick up a homeless man, who delights in serving the hungry at our church soup kitchen, who puts strangers at ease and lifts the burdens of the lonely.

At our church's annual camp last summer, we answered a knock at the door of our camper.

"We just wanted to let you know how much we are enjoying Eric," said a smiling woman, accompanied by her husband.

I motioned the couple to come in and sit down.

For the next 15 minutes, they shared what an encouragement our eight-year-old boy had been to their family. Their son, Steven, was blind, and Eric had a sixth sense for looking out for him. He made sure the boy was included in all the camp activities and accepted on the playground by the other children.

As the couple made their way back to their own camper, we thought of the ways our energetic son was enriching other people's lives—and not least of all, our own.

Need Help?

If you are wondering whether your child has ADHD, or how you can get help, contact CHADD for a referral to professionals in your community. The address: CHADD, 499 NW 70th Ave., Suite 308, Plantation, FL 33317; or phone (305) 587-3700.

Sandra Doran, an author and seminar speaker, is currently a doctoral student specializing in ADHD.

❧ 24

When My
Worst Fear
Came True

*Dianne Smith**

Seventeen years ago, my husband, Mike, and I moved from Southern California to the White Mountains of northeast Arizona. We had just begun our family. In that sleepy, little town—population 2,000—we felt confident we could raise our children in peace and safety.

For years, we did enjoy the quiet community, and we even launched a successful business there. Life was serene and relatively uneventful until one April afternoon two years ago.

That day seemed ordinary as I hurried about my household activities. Everywhere I went, I was accompanied by my fifth child, three-year-old Tiffany.

Tiffany was our "surprise package," arriving six years after our other children. This tiny girl's sweet smile and bubbly personality made her the family favorite. Tiff was adored by all of us.

As the afternoon progressed, my daughter and I chatted as we folded clothes. I launched into my "concerned mother" routine, casually asking Tiffany a question I had directed at one time or another to all of my children.

"Has anyone ever touched your private area, Tiff?"

She nodded yes.

"Who?" I demanded, nausea gripping my stomach.

"Wesley," came her quiet answer.

Wesley. The 12-year-old boy I had hired to look after Tiffany several afternoons a week while I worked at my home-based business. I had always been home while they played together.

Don't panic, Dianne, I calmed myself. *Perhaps Tiffany is mistaken.*

But, as I questioned her further, I realized no three-year-old could invent the disgusting details Tiff was relating to me.

Decisively, I gathered my purse and my daughter and headed straight to the police. Six months before, I had read this advice—immediately contact authorities—in a magazine article on child molestation. Little did I realize that this horror would soon invade my own life.

At the police station, Tiffany was taken into a different room for questioning. The authorities had been taught specific procedures to pull the facts out of a small child with a limited vocabulary. Afterward, they suggested I call a friend to take Tiffany home while they spoke privately with me.

In their office, the officers disclosed the extent of Tiffany's victimization. Not only had my three-year-old been sexually molested over a week's time, but she had also been raped.

"No! It can't be true!"

Right in their office, I began to scream. I yelled and carried on, never wanting to stop. When I finished reacting, I knew I'd have to face the reality of what had happened to my precious child.

In my heart, I didn't want to believe it. *How could a 12-year-old boy do this?* I thought. *Didn't boys that age fill their minds with thoughts of BMX bikes, baseball cards, and Nintendo games? Where had Wesley come up with these vile ideas?*

Dealing with the Aftermath

That evening, when the police questioned Wesley at his home, the boy admitted to everything.

Meanwhile, I took Tiffany to a woman gynecologist, who medically confirmed that the rape had occurred. My daughter immediately began seeing a counselor, beginning the process of working through the trauma.

But I couldn't get over what that boy had done to my innocent little girl. Resentment dominated me. I blamed Wesley for the hurt he'd caused our family.

"He's shattered an innocent girl's life," I said to myself. "Wesley deserves to be punished."

I began to build a case against him, imagining ways to hurt Wesley. Friends, even Christians, justified my vengeful spirit. But because of my spiritual upbringing, deep inside I recognized that there was one important element missing from the tragedy—God's grace.

Oh, it was there. I knew that from His Word and past experience, but it was difficult to feel His grace amidst such devastating turmoil.

One day, as a friend drove Tiffany and me to a counseling session, she remarked, "Well, Dianne, welcome to the 'Poor-Broken-Slob Club.' Now you can see if your words really work."

I knew what she was referring to.

For years I had been active in a pro-life ministry, counseling post-abortion victims. From the outside looking in, I had experienced other women's abortions, desertions, and abuse. I always counseled with positive words and Scripture. Lives had been changed while trusting Romans 8:28: "And we know that in all things God works for the good of those who love him. . . ."

Now Tiffany's life had been broken. I was certain no good would ever come from my small child's victimization. In my heart, I knew I was capable of deep hatred. However, in counseling embittered women, I had learned what internal venom could do. I knew it could destroy both my relationship with God and my family. I wasn't strong enough to stop the hating, but I knew God was.

At this point, I didn't feel ready to forgive Wesley. But out of past experience, I knew I had to trust God to use the worst in my life to glorify Himself and benefit others.

With this belief, I whispered a simple, stumbling prayer: "God, don't let me hate."

In my mind, I envisioned a chasm as deep as the Grand Canyon filled with my bile. I saw myself standing on the brink, slipping fast. I knew if I fell in, my joyful, victorious Christian life would be over.

I pleaded again, "God, don't let me step over that edge. Please hold me back."

Even after I prayed, I still wrestled with my emotions. But for the first time in two months, I felt some peace as I allowed God's grace to sustain me.

Cause and Effect

The following September, the court date arrived for Wesley's sentencing. I had wondered how a 12-year-old boy could come up with the atrocities Wesley had. My answer came as his counselor revealed his findings.

Pornography.

At a vulnerable age and a crucial time in Wesley's life—as his parents were experiencing marital problems—the youth had been introduced to hard-core pornographic materials at a summer camp. It was only a matter of time before Wesley acted out what he had seen.

During the court proceedings, Mike and I were allowed to share our grief.

Unable to contain his tears, my husband said, "I will never be able to look at a little girl again without wondering if this terrible thing has happened to her, too."

Standing next to Mike, I poured out my heart. Putting the incident from my mind seemed impossible, especially in our small town where we'd run into Wesley at social events or even the grocery store. Seeing him had even triggered a reaction from Tiffany, the therapist reported. Tiff had begun acting out the molestation with her dolls.

I concluded my statement by pleading with the family to move. "I can't stand the thought of living in the same town and seeing this boy all the time."

When I sat down, the judge called Wesley and his mother to the bench and asked if they had anything to say. The boy stammered as he apologized for his actions, adding, "I've lost all my friends."

His broken mother, weeping openly, expressed her own hurt and remorse over her son's crime.

"Our lives have been shattered," she cried. "This is my son, and I love him. Yet what he has done is so terrible. I know how Mrs. Smith's heart is broken because my heart is broken, too."

Suddenly at that moment, I saw the woman through a mother's eyes. Realizing that her life had also been devastated, I prayed my third prayer: "Lord, help me to forgive."

God had kept me from stepping off the edge into hatred. Now I desperately needed His help to set both Wesley and me free. The Lord honored my request, and I was acutely aware that the mercy I was feeling was a gift from God.

The judge cleared his throat, then sentenced Wesley to two weeks of residential counseling. (Later, we discovered this was a controversial secular program where the youngsters were exposed to more hard-core porn while outfitted with a sensor. If they showed an arousal, they were made to sniff ammonia as a deterrent. After this "therapy," he would be released on probation until age 18.)

After pronouncing sentence, the judge announced to the courtroom, "I am giving this boy the strongest sentence I can under the law."

As the gavel came down to dismiss the case, I whispered to Joanne, with the Victim's Assistance Department, "I'd like to have a word with Wesley."

"No, I don't want you to, Dianne." Her voice was firm. "It's best if the two parties don't interact. I've actually seen fistfights take place."

After assuring Joanne that would not happen, I hurried over to Wesley and his mother. When I reached them, I hugged each one.

Looking Wesley straight in the eye, I told him, "Nothing will ever take away the pain you have caused our family. But, I want you to know something, Wesley. Because of Jesus Christ and His love for all of us, I am able to fully forgive you."

As I returned to my family, I overheard Joanne comment, "Well, I'll be! In all my years in this work, I've never seen anything like that in this courtroom!"

Later, Wesley's mother told me if I hadn't expressed forgiveness to her son, she knew he could never fully recover from his crime.

I still pray for Wesley, that his restoration will be complete, as mine has been. Oh, the pain is still there, but the hatred and vengeance are gone. God has placed peace in my heart instead. He was able to use our family's tragedy for His glory, and hopefully, to help others.

Moving Past the Pain

Some months later, I flew to Washington, D.C., to speak at a meeting of the "Enough Is Enough" anti-pornography campaign. This group of women from varying backgrounds are seeking to reduce sexual violence and to prevent women and children from becoming victims of harmful pornography.

I testified (without using my last name) that porn brought unforgettable harm to a three-year-old girl—and a 12-year-old boy. I pleaded that our nation's lawmakers would wake up and work to eliminate child pornography and illegal hard-core porn from the open market.

It's been two years since my daughter's molestation. Recently, I took her to the therapist who has worked with her since the incident. Her words brought joy and relief to my heart.

"Your daughter is doing wonderfully," she said. "She's happy and adjusting well. She doesn't need to continue therapy at this time." I learned that I had to be aware that during several development stages, a few sessions could be helpful so recurring memories don't overwhelm her.

As a mother, I continue to pick up the pieces of my shattered life, trying to move past this point of pain. As I do, I take with me the assurance that God's grace—His undeserved love and forgiveness—will be my traveling companion.

🌺 🌺 🌺

Child Molestation: What to Look For, What to Do

In Dianne's case, a mother's worst fear became reality: child sexual abuse. The thought is so repulsive most parents won't even consider it.

But, according to some studies, anywhere from 25 percent to 66 percent of girls and 25 percent to 50 percent of boys will be sexually molested by age 18. As Dianne discovered, the tragedy of child sexual abuse can happen to any family.

There are, however, certain tip-offs in your child's behavior that would indicate a need to get further information, or check it out with a counselor:

- Sexually "acting out": sex play with dolls or toys, drawing naked bodies, speaking or acting seductively, or instances of sexual aggression
- Behavioral changes at home and school, such as withdrawal or rebelliousness, a feeling that "something is not quite right"
- Sleep disturbances and increased nightmares
- Bed-wetting
- Clinging—fear of being left alone
- Depression
- Lack of appetite
- Psychosomatic illnesses

If you discover, like Dianne, that your child has been victimized, here are some important actions to take:

1. *Listen calmly without reaction.* Reassure your child as he or she talks.

2. *Write down exactly what your child says* and include dates. Record any unusual behavior that might confirm the incident. Quote your child word for word.

3. *Go to the authorities.* School officials, police, or your family doctor are trained in this area.

4. *Assure your child* that neither the abuse nor its outcome is his or her fault.

5. *Respond to your child's fears*; don't disregard them.

6. *Permit him or her to talk*, but don't force it. Sometimes a child will refuse or deny earlier statements due to confused, painful feelings.

7. *Realize that your child may not have negative feelings* about the abuse, and may perceive it as affection.

8. *Offer therapy*, but don't insist on it until the child is ready and feels comfortable with the counselor. If possible, choose a Christian counselor who will honor your family's values.

To provide your children with some extra protection against victimization, here are some suggestions:

• Establish open communication with your children on every subject, even uncomfortable ones like sex and anatomy.

• Be a concerned friend to your child, listening to him and taking him seriously.

• Teach your child to say "no." Sometimes "good kids" haven't been taught to set boundaries or follow their instincts. They want to be polite.

• Tell your children that if something feels wrong to them, it's okay to make a scene—hit, kick, bite, scream, or run. You want them to avoid danger by doing whatever is necessary.

• Give your children a lesson on right and wrong touching. Tell them no one has the right to touch them in a way that makes them feel uncomfortable, no matter who it is. Major video stores offer free community service videos that teach "appropriate touching."

• Proper words are "No one is allowed to touch your private areas." Don't say, "Never let someone touch you." This puts the responsibility on the child, where it doesn't belong.

• No matter who they are with, don't leave children unattended for long; check in on them at various intervals. Molestations by friends or relatives are more common than by strangers. Abuse can occur in a matter of minutes, and usually a child won't cry out or even tell you afterward.

• Work on having a solid family and home. Give your children the affection, attention, and recognition they crave. A pedophile often targets needy kids in problem situations.

Give our children the protection they deserve by sending out the message, "Enough is enough!"

—*Cynthia Culp Allen*

❀ ❀ ❀
Where to Go

The "Enough Is Enough" campaign is a project of the National Coalition Against Pornography. For information or additional resources, write: N-CAP, 800 Compton Rd., Suite 9924, Cincinnati, OH 45231, or call (513) 521-6227.

---

* The names used in this article have been changed to protect their identities.

25

My Very Special Son

Carlene K. Mattson

t the end of a long work day in 1971, I watched six men with Down syndrome step into the crosswalk in front of my car. Twelve curved hands clutched a single rope. As they passed, I could see their protruding tongues and awkward gaits. Most of all, I saw the rope that robbed them of adult dignity and announced their dependence to every onlooker.

I ached with pity. Had God made an error? Had He been looking the other way when something caused their differences?

As a child, I hadn't known very many disabled people. The only instruction I got was "don't stare at them"—a message I found confusing. Did it mean I shouldn't be rude? Were the disabled too awful to look at? And why was everyone so uncomfortable? Were their conditions contagious?

I pushed the scene of the men with Down syndrome away and didn't think about it for a long time. Then on June 9, 1979, the birth of our second son, Jeff, thrust me into their circle.

My pregnancy had been as uneventful as the one for Jeff's older brother, 21-month-old Ty. Because our baby's disability was not identified at delivery, my husband, Bob—who had coached me through an easy labor—went home to make excited calls to our families.

I was still in the recovery room when the on-duty pediatrician stopped by. Instead of coming to my side, he stood at the foot of my gurney.

"Your son has 10 fingers and 10 toes, and his plumbing works," he began. I braced myself because I knew a "but . . . " was coming. "But he has Down syndrome."

I suppose my stunned silence caused the doctor to think I couldn't comprehend his words. He then methodically repeated everything as if I, too, might be retarded.

The news caused my entire body to vibrate uncontrollably, and the attending nurse lovingly put her arm across my shoulder. Her sharing of my grief literally anchored me to the gurney.

What Now?

The doctor finished with the best advice anyone could have given me at that moment: "Just take him home and love him." Then he turned abruptly away.

Later, I would remember his words with thankfulness as I heard about insensitive doctors who had referred to other children as "mongoloid idiot," "too handicapped to take home," or even "shark bait."

Lying alone in the hospital room, I felt the isolation of being different. My baby, only minutes old, had just been labeled mentally retarded. I begged God to make the doctor's diagnosis a mistake. Maybe he had confused my baby with another's. . . . Maybe he talked to the wrong mother.

The next day I went home from the hospital, but Jeff did not. He had become jaundiced and was placed in an incubator under a special light. Between shuttling to the hospital to feed Jeff and caring for Ty, I ordered books on Down syndrome from the closest university medical library. Instead of being helpful, the dated books typecast people with Down syndrome as a species unto themselves. I tearfully muddled my way through those initial days, dealing with the realization that the child we dreamed about during my pregnancy was not the baby I had delivered.

My attitude changed one evening when I returned to the hospital to nurse Jeff. He was the only baby in the nursery who had been left unattended. He had wiggled out of his protective eye mask and was lying in his own excrement because he wasn't wearing a diaper. I suddenly stopped feeling sorry for myself. I realized Jeff needed a mother who was not focusing on her own loss. Whether he was neglected by design or by accident, that evening marked a turning point for me.

At home, I got out my yellow pages, looked under "handicapped," and began dialing numbers. Finally, one of the organizations put me in touch with a support group for parents of children with Down syndrome. Knowing they had walked in my shoes and were faring well was an incredible comfort. My feelings of isolation melted away.

The Real Truth

My experiences have probably not been too different from what you imagine. You, too, may have felt pity for the handicapped and would be saddened to give birth to a child with mental retardation. What is staggering to people who have not had my experiences is how temporary those emotions are.

What made Jeff's birth so painful was all the preconceived ideas I had about people with disabilities; in short, my own prejudice. If I had only been aware of all the things that people with disabilities can achieve, I would have felt admiration and never pity. Misinformed, I thought the lives of the developmentally disabled were hopeless, a "life on a rope" existence. I was wrong.

I also believed my child would be different from everyone else. He is not. He is more like you than unlike you. He has red hair, a batch of freckles, and an endearing, dimpled smile. He has hopes and dreams and a wonderful ability to form thriving relationships. I love to see the world he sees—a world surrounded with wonder.

I wish someone could have told me what a treasure I had just been given upon the birth of this little fellow, instead of relating horror stories about institutionalized adults. I remember the excitement on Jeff's face the first time his father fingered his favorite song on our new piano, or the winsome way he asks me to close my eyes before he gives me a gift. He joyously brings me pocketfuls of dandelions and sniffs a gazania with such zest that his nose turns orange from the pollen.

Jeff is thankful for the smallest kindness, and he sees beauty in ways I miss, even to the velvet moss growing in a sidewalk crack. Because other kids are quicker, Jeff rarely gets to the swings or the drinking fountain first, but his tolerance for those who rush past him excels those of his faster peers.

My son's diagnosis dredged up my greatest fears, but his spirit exceeds my greatest dreams. He delights in looking into the eyes of every baby he meets, and he takes time each evening to recap all he is thankful for in his prayers.

Looks from Friends

People who don't know Jeff feel sorry for me. I've yet to introduce myself to someone and mention that my second son has Down syndrome and not get looks of sympathy. People find it hard to believe that he is so valuable and such an asset to our family. A short while after Jeff came into our lives, my husband and I were discussing heaven and what Jeff would be like there. In the hereafter, would Jeff be the boy he would have been on earth if he hadn't had an extra piece of genetic material?

Suddenly in this personal pondering, sorrow came over us. Could perfection in heaven mean we would be looking at eternity without Jeff as we know him? In that momentary sadness, we realized we preferred him just the way he was. Once I had fervently beseeched God to change my baby. Instead He changed me.

The greatest obstacle to being handicapped—or challenged, or disabled, or whatever label we may be using this year—is not the condition, but the stigma society still associates with it. We live in a broken world, and we imperfect people are always devaluing those different from ourselves. The truth is we are valuable because of who we are, not because of how we look or what we accomplish. And that applies to all of us, the disabled and the temporarily able-bodied alike.

I'm convinced God didn't turn His back at the moment of Jeff's conception. He is still the God of miracles and capable of healing anyone. However, in this instance, the one who received healing was me. Our Lord is still in the business of changing lives, but not always in the ways we expect.

Several years ago, Jeff played in a special Little League for kids with disabilities. After many seasons of watching from the bleachers and rooting while his big brother played ball, Jeff's opportunity finally arrived. When he received his uniform, he couldn't wait to get home to put it on. When he raced out from his bedroom, fully suited up, he announced to me, "Mom, now I'm a real boy!" Though his words pushed my heart to my throat, I assured him he had always been a "real boy."

Of course, I recognized what Jeff was telling me. He, all too often, has felt the emotions one experiences when others see only your handicap and forget to see you. He knew that this uniform meant for him a small step toward being more like other boys his age.

My hope in sharing my experiences is that you will set aside any prejudices and look past the differences of the disabled. By doing so, you can help make this a kinder world for Jeff to grow up in. And for some unborn children, it might mean being allowed to grow up at all.

Next time, if you see us out and about, look closely. You even have my permission to stare, but if you do, please notice something. I'm the one who is "different," and Jeff is the "real boy."

Carlene K. Mattson and her family live in Laguna Hills, California.

26

The Day the Heartbeat Stopped

Kathleen B. Nielson

*L*ast February, on a cold, cloudy morning, I walked briskly into my OB/GYN's office for a routine checkup. Pregnant 16 weeks, I was just emerging from three months of nausea and fatigue.

On this day, however, I felt energetic and excited about a fourth child joining our family, happy to see my body stretching with the new life inside me. The week before, I had even felt those first few flutterings that pregnant women anticipate. I have always found pregnancy to be a consumingly happy experience, full of mystery and joy.

I signed in on the clipboard, took a seat with six or seven other women, and discreetly eyed the larger-bellied ones, trying to imagine getting that big again. I anticipated a quick four-month checkup, highlighted by a rush of delight that would come when the baby's heartbeat suddenly gushed and pulsed audibly through the stethoscope held to my stomach. After the appointment, two precious hours of reading and writing awaited me before my afternoon car pool duties. It would be a good day.

After waiting almost an hour, however, I hopped onto the examining table with a frown of frustration. In a businesslike way, my doctor took the stethoscope from his pocket and began to move it across my stomach, up and down, slowly, side to side, then up and down again . . . an intense silent treasure hunt. Several minutes passed.

An ironic sense of replay tugged at me: Four weeks earlier, the stethoscope had amplified only the rumblings and gurglings of my own body. An immediate ultrasound then had answered my fears by showing an active little fetus with discernible arms and legs and a steadily pulsing heart. I had taken home the ultrasound photographs, pored over them with my husband, Niel, and our three boys, then proudly mailed them to my parents and parents-in-law.

Now, as I lay on the examination table, the heartbeat should have been clearly coming through. After a few more minutes of careful searching, the doctor put away his stethoscope. Remarking that perhaps the baby was in an awkward position, he led me into the office ultrasound room. Such stillness, such dead quiet filled that place as the doctor and nurse directed the test. I could see the screen, and I could trace the baby's wonderfully developed form. Apparently, it was just the right size for 16 weeks gestation.

But it was motionless. No little circle pulsed at the center. Nothing squirmed.

"There's no heartbeat, is there?"

"No, I'm afraid not," the doctor answered.

He ordered a second ultrasound, this time on a more sophisticated machine in the X-ray unit. Meanwhile, I called Niel, who immediately left work to join me. When he arrived, we listened quietly together to the results of the second ultrasound. The doctor confirmed that the baby was dead and advised inducing labor in the next week to protect my health.

A Lonely Vigil

Over the next several days, as I continued to carry the baby, my sorrow over the baby's death formed a thick, heavy barrier between me and sleep. At night I would creep quietly downstairs, find a sleepy welcome from my huge, gentle mastiff dog, and curl up on the couch with her at my feet and a hymnal and a Bible in my hands.

I roved through Scripture as a desperately hungry person might make her way through the most wonderful smorgasbord. All alone I held out my plate. No one stood ahead for me to watch or help, and no one was behind waiting for me to finish. I tasted this and that verse, stopping to take in each distinct flavor. I tried some of my most favorite morsels of Scripture, and they tasted better than I ever remembered. I tried some more unfamiliar dishes and marveled at their satisfying flavors. I was hungry, and I was deeply filled.

A few passages affected me so vividly that I memorized them, treasuring the experience of saying them over and over to be sure of each word, and then saying them again just to feel their strength at work in me. At a time when I felt a terrible emptiness inside, I inhaled the breath of God by taking Scripture into myself. At a time when I did not know what to say to God, through His Word I was able to open myself to Christ, who in the beginning *was* the Word. At a time of meeting death, even carrying it inside me, I was letting the very life of God into my heart. The Bible's words were the flavor of that life to me, so that I could taste it. They were God's blessing on my head as I was bowed down low, and they lifted me up.

I turned to Psalm 36 the first night after that sad checkup. One passage stopped me:

> O Lord, *you preserve both man and beast.*
> *How priceless is your unfailing love!*

> *Both high and low among men*
> *find refuge in the shadow of your wings;*
> *They feast on the abundance of your house;*
> *you give them drink from your river of delights.*
> *For with you is the fountain of life;*
> *in your light we see light.*

(Psalm 36:6b-9)

I looked again at the phrase, "O Lord, you preserve both man and beast" and pondered long over it.

God didn't preserve my baby, I thought.

But then in a rush I knew God *had* preserved my baby, in His own way that is higher than mine, in His "priceless, unfailing love." He had taken my son to Himself and would preserve him pure and holy forever. My child was "in the shadow of God's wings," "feasting on the abundance of God's house" and "drinking from his river of delights." Knowing my baby would be cared for and delighted by God Himself comforted me immensely.

During the four days of waiting, I gradually gave my child into the care of God. And yet, I kept praying for a miracle. Three more ultrasounds were performed, and during each one I silently poured out my heart, pleading for my baby's life. I knew my Lord could give life if He chose to do so. When I had no more words, over and over again I asked Jesus to plead for me before God his Father. I kept remembering Martha, who, after her dear brother Lazarus' death, said to Jesus, "I know that even now God will give you whatever you ask."

But God did not choose to answer in the way I so heartily desired. The final, silent ultrasound took place early on a Monday morning as the last step before labor was induced. My beautiful, still, tiny-perfect son was delivered 15 hours later. There in that labor and delivery room, identical to the ones where we had experienced the amazing joy of birth, my husband and I grieved over a child's death. We held him and wept and prayed over him, marveled at his tiny toes, and finally entrusted him to God.

The Peace of God

I write these words not just to tell the facts of my story. Within the sad facts lies another story concerning the healing that took place deep inside me throughout this experience. The healing came from various sources. Many people brought it, especially my husband. Voices on the telephone, quiet visits, home-cooked meals, lovely cards and flowers supported and surrounded our family. Prayers of God's people became almost palpable as they buoyed and balanced us in deep waters.

But as I look back, the healing of God's Word stands central. I have studied the Bible often. I have taught it and written about it. I love its beauty and its truth. Scripture has been my lamp and my armor along many roads. But never before have I so vividly experienced its living, healing work in my life. People talk about *applying* Scripture, that is, making it work practically in concrete experience. In this experience the Holy Spirit *applied* Scripture as a doctor would apply ointment to a wound, bringing about sweet healing in my soul.

The healing began during those first nights of searching the Bible for help and encouragement. The healing continued for many days and weeks and months. Soon after the delivery, for example, my body began to produce milk—a difficult reminder of what had occurred, just as I was doing my best to look ahead and not back. Those verses from Psalm 36 began to echo powerfully: "You give them drink from your river of delights. For with you is the fountain of life." I wept to think I would never feed this baby, but I wept with joy to think that God was nourishing him from His unending river. God had taken him back to the source, the "fountain of life."

Internalizing these verses as I applied them to my child brought me to the further point of applying them to myself. I became again a little child before God, dependent on Him for preservation of life, looking to Him for food and drink. In my heart, I knelt down by that river to drink, and looking up I saw the great fountain from which the river flows. I looked to the face of God and said with all my being, "With You is the fountain of life; in Your light we see light."

Steadily, the light has become brighter. At first, in the weeks after the miscarriage, the sight of other infants in their mothers' arms brought tears. Gradually, that sight brought a marveling, newly tuned wonder at the miracle of how God forms life. Having seen my fourth child and sent him on to God, I now look at my other three boys with more amazement and thankfulness than ever before; God is gracious to preserve them and to preserve us all within the shadow of His wings.

God's light dramatically reveals the darkness of the world around us. Having held in my arms a baby of 16 weeks gestation, I wonder more deeply how millions of women are able to destroy such amazing little human beings. Every day, as I read statistics concerning the planned deaths of babies in the womb, I grieve more intensely and personally over the evil of abortion in our world.

On the day in August when I had expected our fourth child to be born, I could look up to the throne of God with a heart at peace, truly thanking Him for revealing Himself to me ever more deeply through the experience of losing a child. I look forward to meeting that child in heaven. For each day until then, I look with all my faith and energy to God and to His powerful, healing Word.

Kathleen Nielson lives with her husband and three sons in Wheaton, Illinois.

PART FIVE

FOCUS ON
EDUCATION

27

Which School for Your Child?

Ken Wackes
Headmaster of Westminster Academy
in Ft. Lauderdale, Florida

*O*ne of our school's 17-year-old juniors, Amy, was invited to speak at a local church recently. Amy is a bright, articulate, nice-looking girl, and she did a fine job describing the benefits of Westminster Academy to the congregation.

One couple was so impressed that the next day they called their architect and canceled a contract to build their "dream home."

"We've decided to take the money and put our kids in Westminster Academy next fall," the father said. "If Amy is the type of person your school produces, that's what we want for our children."

I see more and more Christian parents choosing a Christian education for their children. Sure, it's a financial sacrifice, especially for young families. At Westminster, tuition ranges from $3,000 a year for elementary school to $5,000 for high school. But I've heard story after story of how God met the financial needs of parents once they chose Christian schooling.

Our tuition is higher than most Christian schools because we pay our teachers on a par with the public school system. Some Christian schools cut corners with salaries and suffer rapid turnover. That does not build a strong school. Sixty-five percent of our teachers have been here 12 years or more.

Our teachers' commitment is one reason why the education we offer equals and often surpasses anything you'll find in public schools. Our class size is small—about 20 students per classroom. We stress pure academics—language arts, reading, and mathematics. We have computer labs, art, music, theater, and physical education. We've produced National Merit scholars and award-winning political clubs. Our football team won the state championship last fall, and our science clubs dominate science fairs. Last year, five graduates left for foreign missionary service.

All day long the students are learning in a Christ-centered environment. In a Christian school, *every* side of an issue—including the spiritual—can be explored and debated. That's forbidden in public schools.

Such was not always the case, however. Before the Civil War, most schooling took place in a church-related environment. Even when towns and communities built common schools with public money, the curriculum was based upon traditional Christian values. That began to change rapidly after World War I.

The Supreme Court's decision in 1962 to ban school prayer signaled the beginning of the end. Today, our public school system doesn't allow God in the classroom. It's gotten so bad that several teachers I know were forbidden to pray together before class while sitting in a car in the school parking lot! Many school districts are even afraid to call Christmas vacation "Christmas vacation." The two-week break is called "winter holiday," while Easter has become "spring break" in many parts of the country.

What I want to stress, however, is that God gave us a *biblical mandate* to provide Christian schooling for our children, no matter how good the public school is perceived to be. Proverbs 22:6 says: "Train a child in the way he *should* go . . ." That doesn't give us permission to deliberately school our children in the way they *shouldn't* go!

Similarly, Deuteronomy 6 commands us to surround our children all day and all night with constant reminders of God's presence and involvement, while Psalm 1 says: "Blessed is the man who does not walk in the counsel of the ungodly. . . ." Only once in the history of the church have Christian parents deliberately placed their children in pagan schools in contradiction to the biblical mandate, and that has been in the 20th century.

An erroneous assumption embraced by our culture and, sadly, by some Christian parents, is that God can be excluded from daily school life entirely—and nothing will be missed! Others believe God has nothing to do with art, history, math, social studies, biology or basketball. Some assume that a child can be adequately equipped in a *secular* setting for a lifetime of *kingdom* work and service.

Actually children are cheated in a school system that excludes God. By law, public schools cannot teach the whole truth about life, and, by deliberate design, textbook companies and teacher unions have purged God from texts and lesson plans. This institutional bias leaves children with huge gaps in their learning that are rarely filled later.

Many parents don't believe this, however, and they've told me that the Great Commission in Matthew 28 calls us to infiltrate the "real" world of public schools with our sons and daughters. Such thinking is nonsense. Here's why:

First of all, the "real" world is where *God* is present and adored. Where He is ignored is the phony world of make-believe. Second, exposing our children to a curriculum handcuffed by a biased legal system and, in many cases, to the pagan influence of a non-Christian teacher who things and operates away from the authority of the Bible is like sending 11- and 12-year-olds into combat. Our troops stationed in foreign outposts are mature, hardened, well-trained servicemen and servicewomen equipped for war. Our children in public schools are fodder for cannons.

No, the Scriptures are clear. Public schools are mission fields for Christian teachers and administrators (and we should encourage and pray for each one), but they're not suitable schooling environments for children of Christian parents.

Why I Believe in Public Schooling

Guy Doud
1986 National Teacher of the Year from Baxter, Minnesota

Since my book, *Molder of Dreams*, was released several years ago, I've done hundreds of radio talk-show interviews. I enjoy talking about my book, my relationship with Christ, and how adults have been molders of *my* dreams.

One time, my seat was barely warm when the first caller charged in. "You can't be a Christian and teach in the public school," he began. "And if you're a Christian, you can't send your children to public school either."

I was taken aback. I wasn't used to people telling me I'm not a Christian. Not only do I teach in a public school, but my children attend public school as well. I guess I struck out on both accounts.

The caller bore in. "The Bible says that if you're not for Him, you're against Him, and since the public schools aren't for Him, they're against Him. Since you're a part of the public school, you're against Him, too, which means you're going to hell!"

In one sweeping generalization, this caller had passed judgment on me, the tens of thousands of Christians who work in the public schools and the millions of parents who send their children to public schools. I was hurt and angry.

"Are you a citizen of the United States?" I asked.

"Yes," he responded.

"Using your reasoning, you're not a Christian either."

"What do you mean?"

"Well, sir, although there are many Christians in the United States—just as there are many Christians in the public schools—the United States is not a 'Christian country.' Consequently, if the United States is not officially for Him, we're against Him. Since you're a part of the United States, you're against Him, too. That means you're going to hell."

"That's absurd!" he shouted.

"It sure is," I quickly agreed, trying hard not to match his volume. Then the talk-show host broke in and said we had another caller. I was happy to move on.

The next person had a different angle. She said she and her husband had sent their children to several different Christian schools, but found something objectionable in each one. The first school, she said, tried to indoctrinate her children with the tenets of their denominational beliefs. "They told our kids that unless they believed *this* about baptism and *that* about the Holy Spirit, they weren't saved. Our kids came home confused. We put them in another Christian school, but the kids picked on them. That school was very cliquish.

"We tried two more Christian schools: One didn't have many extracurricular activities for the kids, and at the last one, the headmaster was found guilty of sexually abusing one of the students." She paused. "So we put our children in the local public school. They just love it. Both my husband and I are involved in the parents' organization, and we've met many other wonderful Christian parents."

The host of the radio program asked me for a response.

"We don't want to give people the impression that Christian

schools are known for abuse," I replied. "Nor should we assume all
public schools are problem-free. The bottom line is that it is not right
to make broad generalizations."

And that's the way I feel. So much depends on the school, the
parents and the children. All public schools aren't bad. All Christian
schools aren't good. All home schooling isn't done because parents
are withdrawn from society. It's dangerous to the cause of Christ for
Christians to engage in such quick judgments.

I also resent it when people harshly judge the public school
system. After all, a public school teacher led me to Jesus Christ as my
personal Savior. But I'm the first to admit public schools have problems—lots of problems. I also believe, however, that many problems
exist in the homes and the churches of America. I'm not about to
give up on the family or the church, nor am I ready to give up on our
public schools.

For the most part, public schools offer more for the student,
including competitive sports, extracurricular activities and advanced
curriculum—especially in the areas of math and science.

The greater good can be served when Christian parents keep
their children in the local school and work to make those schools
even better.

In Matthew 25:40, Jesus said: "Whatever you do to the least of
these my brethren, so you do unto me." What about the "least of
these" who will never have any alternative other than to attend
public schools? Don't we need to make public schools the best we
can for them? If we love Jesus, we must look beyond our own children to those who have no one to care for them.

I encourage you to get involved in your local school district. You
will discover people who really care about kids. Mothers should consider joining—or starting—a "Moms in Touch" prayer group, because
prayer works wonders in our schools.

In the public schools, you'll also find dedicated Christians serving
Christ. True, they cannot openly "preach" to children, but nothing
prevents them from living out their faith before the students.

Numerous Christian parents are involved in their children's educations. They know what's going on in the classrooms and they're working to change the curriculum where needed. By their commitment, they're not only part of an exciting mission field, but they're touching lives for eternity.

Chuck Colson once said, "Be a witness for Christ. If necessary, use words." The countless thousands of Christians who teach in the public schools are powerful witnesses for Jesus Christ. They realize that the best way to brighten the darkness is not to condemn it, but to shine a light in it.

Why I Believe in Home Schooling

Susan Beatty
Co-founder of the Christian Home Educators Association of
California, headquartered in Anaheim.

*F*or the past nine years, our children, Joel, Melanie, and Tony, have answered the phone with "The King's Academy." And well they should. They're being educated at home.

I first heard about home schooling on a "Focus on the Family" broadcast in 1982. Dr. Dobson interviewed an education expert who listed symptoms of burnout in third-grade schoolchildren. He was describing Joel, our first-grader! In preschool and kindergarten, he had been well behaved, but now he was wandering around the classroom, unable to pay attention.

Our child is already ruined, I thought. But as I researched child development, I discovered it wasn't too late.

As my husband, Larry, and I talked and prayed, we realized *we* were responsible for our children's education and that *we* could offer them more than traditional schools could. We also realized we weren't facing just an educational issue but a spiritual one. Without hesitation, we took Joel out of school and started working with him at home.

We've never regretted our decision. But along the way, we've found that many people have misconceptions about home schooling. New friends think our children—15, 12s and 9—slough off much of the day. But we keep a regular schedule.

Our school day begins at 9:00 with Bible study and prayer. Grammar and vocabulary exercises follow, along with assignments for Friday's history lesson. After lunch, they finish their work and read.

Wednesday afternoons are for group activities with other home schoolers. Sometimes we have a park day or take a field trip.

On Friday, the children from several families meet at one home for history. The moms divide the responsibilities: one leads devotions, one teaches the main lesson, and another takes the accompanying hands-on activity, such as supervising the making of salt-dough maps or costumes for a historical play the students write. I'm responsible for "Culture," so after lunch I lead the children through an assignment in writing, literature, or music. When we were studying ancient Rome, we read *Julius Caesar*. For a study of ancient India, the students wrote a play and performed it for their fathers in the evening. Presently, they're working on a major research paper, complete with note cards, outline, and first draft.

We're confident our children are getting a good education. Recently, the National Center for Home Education checked the academic progress of homeschooled students. They found that the average student scored above the 80th percentile on national achievement tests, such as the Stanford Achievement or Iowa Basic Skills. The average public school score, of course, is the 50th percentile.

Another comment we hear is, "But what about socialization?" Our 12-year-old daughter is involved in three singing ministries. Our youngest son works with the church puppet ministry. We've also been involved with Little League and gymnastics.

Occasionally, a mother of traditionally schooled youngsters asks me how I can stand having my children home all day. I don't see that as a chore—it's a privilege. God has given us the responsibility for our children, and when we stand before Him to give an account, He's going to ask how we handled it. He has established families as the center of society. Strong families result in a strong society.

We need to ask ourselves, "Why does a child need an education?" The world tells us one thing; Scripture tells us another. If you've thought through your biblical responsibility before the Lord and can fulfill it through a traditional school, that's fine. But my husband and I believe such schools have replaced the final authority of the parents. The best way we can educate our children is through one-on-one tutoring.

I've had people tell me to put my children in a traditional school in order to prepare them for "real life." The family *is* real life. It contains sickness and sorrow, as well as joy and laughter. All the emotions in the outside world are in the microcosm of the home.

Other moms say they'd love to home school, but they can't because of younger children. Granted, that makes it more difficult, but not impossible. The six-year-old doesn't need to be on an all-day lesson schedule. Often he needs just an hour of "formal" education. You can teach the rest through informal projects such as baking cookies, cleaning, and gardening—things that are going on in the home anyway. You just need to look at the activity with an eye for turning it into a learning experience.

Many mothers worry that if they home school, they won't have time to do all their housework. You can't do it all. I've learned that while the children are young, a spotless house and gourmet meals every night just aren't important. The children's education ranks higher than a waxed floor.

We see increasing numbers of fathers who are finding ways to work at home so they can be part of the family during the day. Strong family relationships aren't easily attainable when everyone is going 19 different directions during the day and coming home for just a couple hours each evening—if that long. And with weekends consumed by chores, church, and social activities, when does a family have time to develop important relationships? Home schooling readily provides a way.

My husband and I are committed to educating our children at home because we believe God has called us to do this. If we don't have a plan, our children will turn out like everyone else. We believe God has called His people to be out of the ordinary.

28

I Need More than an Apple a Day

Jane Ardelean

*I*t's a muggy July afternoon here in Tennessee, with the thick air hovering over the Cumberland river valley. But I ignore the suffocating heat as I sort through my lesson books and think about the students who will be entering my fourth-grade classroom in just a few weeks.

Some I already know, since this will be my fifth year in a brick, one-story building that houses 600 pupils. Most of them will come from middle-class and professional homes, but 15 percent will arrive from a housing project at the town's edge. No matter what the students' economic status, however, I know their needs will basically be the same—knowledge, security, and love.

223

As I thumb through last year's roll book, I think of other students from my 25 years of teaching, which includes stints in Michigan and even Brazil. In my mind, the children crowd around my desk, clamoring to tell me about a new baby brother, a loose tooth, or last night's TV program. Some don't talk, but shyly smile as they rest their hand on my shoulder, just wanting to be close.

When I first started teaching in the late 1960s, our nation's families, for the most part, were intact. Today only a fourth of the students live with both natural parents. The others are living in single-parent or stepparent families. Some even live with their grandparents.

I remember a time when I was teaching in a country school. My second-graders were reading about a family going on a vacation when the father stopped to read the road map. Trying to involve the students in the story, I asked, "Does your dad read a map before you go on a trip?"

Their little faces were thoughtful—and I knew immediately I shouldn't have asked that question. These were rural children, poor for the most part, and they didn't take trips. But just as I started to go on with the lesson, one seven-year-old girl brightened.

"Yes!" she exclaimed. "One time we were driving, and my daddy stopped to look at a map."

Another girl jerked her head toward her.

"Well, he's not your daddy anymore. He's my daddy now, and now he's your uncle."

The light went out of the first little girl's eyes.

I think of the two sisters who have different last names because they have different dads. Now their mother has a new last name because she has a new husband.

I've often wondered if these children—and countless others like them—haven't lost some of the potential they had at birth. These days, they have to think in new ways and adjust to new situations. A few months ago, I was called to give a court statement because one of my students was making trouble between her divorced parents. At a young age, she had already learned how to play them against one another.

New Battles

Children used to be afraid of the Bomb. Now as they hear of the destruction of the rain forest and watch the fish die in their own nearby rivers, they're afraid pollution will destroy their world. And many fear abuse—physical and sexual.

Just a couple of years ago, the fathers of three of my students were in jail because of incest. It helped to know that the abusers were out of the homes, but I wondered if there were other situations I didn't know about. Then one morning, Brenda, a shy youngster who always looked at me through hair that fell across her eyes, stopped by my desk.

"My dad's going to jail today for sexually abusing a child," she whispered.

Before I could catch my breath, she added, "That child was me."

She scurried to her seat. I wanted to put my head down on my desk and sob.

I thought of the grandmother who turned in her son-in-law for abusing his two children. I thought of the local video store with the X-rated room in the back. I refuse to go even into the front section since a third-grader was abused after his father watched those videos.

One winter afternoon I studied the stooped shoulders of timid little Brenda and thought of all that her father had stolen from her. I had been powerless to protect her. What possible good was I doing for these students? In my years in the classroom, had I really helped anyone?

I thought of my own elementary teachers. They had given me a sense of security and an appreciation for music and literature. Once, I wrote them to express my belated thanks—except for the music teacher who had been killed in an auto accident. I'll always regret that I never let her know what she had done for me.

Thinking about the ways my teachers had helped me made my sense of inadequacy worse. One evening, I poured out my hurt. "Lord, year after year, I keep teaching and keep battling the same problems. I need to know that somebody cares about what I do."

A few nights later, I received a call. "This is your favorite fourth-grade student ever," the deep masculine voice said.

I thought for a moment and then asked, "Was that in Michigan, Brazil, or Tennessee?"

He laughed and identified himself as a student from South America. When my husband, Paul, and I were in Brazil, we taught in a jungle school near the Bolivian border for a year. We also spent 10 years at an American school in Brasilia, the capital. The young caller, Danny, was the son of missionaries, and he had been assigned to my classroom in the early 1980s.

Now he was in his second year at Taylor University in Indiana. As we talked about those days in Brazil and the other students in his class, he recalled numerous good times we'd had. I was thrilled he would call an old teacher, but beyond that, his call provided the encouragement I desperately needed.

Road Maps and Mittens

As I look for ways to make a difference in my students' lives, I realize many situations aren't unique to just today's classroom. When I've taught in poor areas, those students could have come right out of the Depression years. But they didn't. It still astonishes me that children in one of the richest nations in the world have such emotional and physical needs.

This past spring, I tried calling one of my fellow teachers to see if she was back from her trip. Her answering machine was filled. Later when I asked her about it, she nodded. "Yes, Karen called me every day and left the same message: 'I love you, Miss Chapman. You're just like a mommy to me.'"

That little second-grader is living with her great-grandmother. Her father had deserted the family when the child was a toddler, then her mother died last year—just before Christmas. The only family member left to care for her was the great-grandmother, who is in her late 70s. Every day, my friend has numerous opportunities to encourage and love that little girl.

Thoughts of that child bring images of others. I remember one early wintry day when one of my students raced to go out for recess. I couldn't help but notice Connie's red, chapped hands. "Didn't you bring your mittens?" I asked.

She shook her head, so I handed her mine and insisted she put them on.

After recess was over, she approached me, smiling and holding her hands in front of her. "Teacher, they're warm!" It hit me that she had never worn mittens before.

When I told one of my friends in Michigan about Connie wearing mittens for the first time, she promptly cleaned out her closets and sent me the winter clothing her children had outgrown. She also told some friends at church, and they collected coats and mittens as well.

One of her friends sent 30 Christmas presents. She hadn't asked how many children I had in my classroom that year, but apparently she asked the Lord: When I opened the box, I discovered 16 toy cars and 14 dolls—exactly what I needed for my 16 boys and 14 girls.

The next day I handed out the gifts, explaining they were sent from a lady in Michigan. One sad little girl had been living with her family in a trailer warmed by a small space heater. As she unwrapped her gift, her eyes shone. "Mrs. Ardelean, I feel so happy today!" It was her first doll.

Those poor rural students still tug at my heart, but the children I taught in a Michigan Christian school weren't free from problems either. I remember the fifth-grader whose father had died the year before from brain cancer. In one of our lessons that day, we were talking about exercising. The boys immediately started talking about fathers who ran or jogged or lifted weights. My heart sank as I saw Jason sitting there, unable to take part in the conversation. Finally he quietly said, almost to himself, "My dad flies now."

I found myself trying to give more love to him that year.

Pointing the Way

When Paul and I taught in the American Embassy school, we weren't allowed to present one faith over another since our classrooms held so many different nationalities and religions. However, I could answer my fourth-graders' questions about how I had celebrated the various holidays back in the States.

The school library had a section on various religions, so when my students asked how Christmas began, I selected an appropriate film. The account began with Christ's birth and ended with His death on the Cross.

One little Hindu boy was amazed. "Imagine that God was born in a stable." A Jewish boy, Stephen, was intrigued. "Teacher, was Jesus really a great *Jew?*"

I assured him that He was.

Stephen was thoughtful for the rest of the afternoon. A few weeks later, he made his father a clay crucifix as a Hanukkah present. When his father opened it, he paused for a long moment and then asked, "Is this what I think it is?"

"Yes," he nodded. "He was a great Jew."

His father smiled and hung the gift in the entrance to their home.

In my mind, I can see Stephen grinning in that way children do when their gift is well received. I also remember the peanut butter jar I received from Rachel, one of my fourth-graders. She had filled it with 31 Bible verses she had chosen and written on slips of paper. For a month, I took one out and read it.

When Rachel's grown, I'll still see her as the delightful 10-year-old who couldn't wait for me to open her gift. I wonder what the Lord has planned for her.

Perhaps that's why Christa McAuliffe, the schoolteacher who perished in *Challenger* space shuttle disaster, said, "I touch the future." I'm convinced that Christian teachers touch not only the future but eternity, too.

As part of my determination to make a difference—now and for eternity—I've set specific goals. Every child is made up of social, physical, academic, emotional, and spiritual parts. I'm convinced that if we don't educate all those areas, we'll produce emotional cripples.

One of the ways I try to touch all those areas is by developing a child's self-worth. At the beginning of the school year, I asked the students if they know what the word *unique* means. As we define it together as "one of a kind," I tell them *they* are one of a kind. I emphasize that no one else in the whole world thinks their thoughts or has their family—and that God made them very special. I try to get them excited about that.

I also try to be positive in the classroom. It's easy for the teacher to be critical with all the pressures we deal with. That's one of the reasons I try to make my classroom attractive as well as safe. Not all of the children will notice the bulletin boards—but they'll know if the classroom is an oasis from home problems.

Touch—verbal as well as physical—is important, too. I try to praise them. A teacher should be a cheerleader. "That's great. . . . Your writing is super. . . . I like the way you reacted when he yelled at you." Students need to know they don't have to be an academic giant to receive honest praise.

I've found that if you touch a child on the shoulder, you have a better chance of being heard. At my age I can even give a needed hug occasionally.

I've also found that I can touch my students spiritually when I pray for him or her: *Lord, bless this child. He tries so hard to keep up with the others on the playground, but he just can't. And that's spilling over into how he thinks about himself in the classroom. Strengthen him, Lord. And help me know how to help him.*

Situations like that remind me that I'm teaching because it's fulfilling to nurture children. I never know how they're going to turn out. Someday I may read about a famous person and realize that he or she once sat at the little desk in the corner. But even if a student isn't famous, it's fulfilling to be in town and have them show me their new baby or say hello in the street.

If I regret anything about teaching, it's the fact that all along I've been criticized for being a working mother. (That's always surprised me, because when I went to Brazil and did the same thing as a missionary, I was praised.) What if all the mothers who teach pulled out?

What would our country be?

God puts Christian teachers in the public schools to temper and steady them. Because we are there, the Holy Spirit is there. What would our schools be like if we weren't there to treat our students compassionately, to give them a good education and to pray for them?

The Lord has me in the classroom for a purpose. And I know this is my ministry.

Jane Ardelean and her husband, Paul, live in Evensville, Tennessee.

29

Your Child Can Succeed in Public School!

Cheri Fuller

Joel charged into the kitchen, threw his books on the table, and cried, "I just can't do this."

Earl and Peggy Stewart had recently moved their family of five to Oklahoma City. The two older boys were adapting well, but it was Joel, their sixth-grader, who was their greatest concern.

Joel's elementary years had been academically tough, especially throughout fourth and fifth grades. Now his standardized test scores in math totaled only 15 out of 100, and 27 on language. How could a child facing these learning difficulties cope in a new public school?

Here he was after only one week of school, throwing his books

231

on the kitchen table and giving up.

His words catapulted Peggy into earnest prayer. She knew that somehow, in some way, God would lead her to a solution.

Peggy's answer came as she volunteered in Joel's classroom. By being there each week, she got to know his teachers, was able to see what they expected of him, and how to make the most of the materials they were teaching. She acquired supplemental resources— sheets such as "Reteaching Long Division"—and helped Joel work on them every day after school.

If his assignment was math, they did half of the problems together, and he did the rest himself. Peggy would check his work, and Joel would rework the problems until he understood what he was doing. They also made spelling flash cards, and they often read aloud the science and history textbook pages, using a globe, atlas, and extra books to enliven the material.

That fall Joel entered the science fair. After a family brainstorming session, he decided his project would be on the variation of heat energy absorbed by different colors. The whole family helped gather materials and cheered him on as he worked. They all shared his joy when he took *first place* in his division. Joel, who had always been overshadowed by his high-achieving older brothers, felt his confidence rise.

After his science fair achievement, Joel began to double his study efforts. He decided to "go for the gold" and earn straight A's. By the fourth nine-week period, he did exactly that! But the most improvement was in standardized test scores, which rose *40 to 50* points by the end of the year.

His parents' involvement and the support of his teachers helped Joel develop confidence. He began to think, *I can do it!*

Education: Whose Responsibility?

We all want to see our children succeed in school, whether they go to Christian, private or public schools. Although many Christian parents opt for religious schools and home schooling, 90 percent of all children from American Christian homes are in public schools.

So, how can parents of children in public schools help them succeed? The answer, as the Stewarts discovered, is *parental involvement*. We know from looking at more than 50 research studies that when parents get involved, those schools improve dramatically; their children are more motivated and better behaved in the classroom; their diverse needs are met more effectively; and scores on achievement tests are significantly higher.

Such parents consider their child's education to be *their own personal responsibility*—not the school's. They see teachers and other school personnel as helpers in meeting educational goals for their children. Public school may be where their children obtain part of their education, but the parents provide additional academic enrichment opportunities for the children.

My husband, Holmes, is a builder. Wise parents build relationships with teachers much as Holmes does with his subcontractors (the framers, trim carpenters, plumbers, etc.). When he designs a house, Holmes meets with the "subs" and goes over the plans, letting them know his expectations for their craftsmanship.

While the work is in progress, they often meet at the housing site. If there are problems, they figure out the cause and come up with solutions. But the ultimate responsibility and liability for building the house rests with the builder, for he is the "general contractor."

In similar ways, parents are the directors or general contractors of their children's education. They may have many teachers along the way, but the parents are their primary instructors and guides. Parents "sub out" parts of the educating task, but they must oversee, provide support, and take the initiative to keep in touch.

"Although Allison spends part of her day in a Washington State public school," said parent Bill Mattox, "my wife and I believe we are her most important teachers. It is we, not the principal and teachers, who are ultimately responsible for her education. It is we who will be held accountable to God."

Cheri Fuller has taught both public and private school in the Oklahoma City area where she and her family reside.

✿ ✿ ✿

A Parent's Checklist

- Schedule a teacher conference within the first month of school, as well as each major grading period or semester. Although special times are sometimes scheduled for parents employed outside the home, you may need to take off work to attend the conference. If an employer gives you trouble, suggest that an "ounce of prevention" now may mean less time off the job later.
- Ask the teacher for "Grade Level Expectancies" and a list of the classes' monthly themes.
- Be sure you oversee your children's work and review any graded tests.
- Read the school newsletters.
- If you are a working parent, inform school personnel of your schedule and how to reach you by phone during the school day. Make sure your child knows your work phone number.
- Express appreciation to the teacher several times during the school year.
- Help your child set a time and place for homework. Be sure to provide support, materials, and encouragement.
- Have regular read-aloud times at home, which is especially important for elementary-age children.
- Consider a volunteer opportunity, such as helping out in the classroom, assisting in a school fundraiser, or joining the class on an outing.
- Remember this thought: If you let your children know that school is a very important place and what they learn extends far beyond the classroom, you'll pave the way for an excellent education.

✿ ✿ ✿

A Student's Bill of Rights on a Public School Campus

1. *The right to meet with other religious students.* The *Equal Access Act* allows students the freedom to meet on campus for the purpose

of discussing religious issues.

2. *The right to identify your religious beliefs through signs and symbols.* Students are free to express their religious beliefs through signs and symbols.

3. *The right to talk about your religious beliefs on campus.* Freedom of speech is a fundamental right mandated in the Constitution and does not exclude the school yard.

4. *The right to distribute religious literature on campus.* Distributing literature on campus may not be restricted simply because it is religious.

5. *The right to pray on campus.* Students may pray alone or with others so long as it does not disrupt school activities or is not forced on others.

6. *The right to carry or study your bible on campus.* The Supreme Court has said that only *state directed* Bible reading is unconstitutional.

7. *The right to do research papers, speeches, and creative projects with religious themes.* The First Amendment does not forbid all mention of religion in public schools.

8. *The right to be exempt.* Students may be exempt from activities and class content that contradicts their religious beliefs.

9. *The right to celebrate or study religious holidays on campus.* Music, art, literature, and drama that have religious themes are permitted as part of the curriculum for school activities if presented in an objective manner as a traditional part of the cultural and religious heritage of the particular holiday.

10. *The right to meet with school officials.* The First Amendment to the Constitution forbids Congress to make any law that would restrict the right of the people to petition the government (school officials).

From the book Students' Legal Rights on a Public School Campus, *by J. W. Brinkley and Roever Communications. For more information, write Roever Communications, P.O. Box 136130, Ft. Worth, Texas 76136, or call (816) 238-2000.*

30

Avoiding Report Card Panic

Les Parrott III, Ph.D.

A frightened fifth-grader stood silently before his father, who was sternly reviewing an unsatisfactory report card. Grasping at anything to break the deafening silence, the youngster said, "Do you think those grades are the result of heredity, or could it just be my environment?"

Like every student in a jam, this boy was looking for an excuse. The father was not amused, but the lad had a point.

Parents *do* influence the classroom performance of their children. A 20-year study at Stanford University focusing on parents' reactions to poor grades and their impact on future success published these unequivocal findings: *First, most parents express negative emotions in responding to poor grades. Second, this is the worst reaction possible since it creates greater tension within the child.*

Moms and dads have the potential to help their children succeed in the classroom. I have seen frustrated parents turn report card panic into a positive experience that earned them high marks in parenting. The family is one of education's most important assets, and research suggests that poor grades will get better in time if the following tools are used by caring parents:

Provide an Emotional Safety Net

During the early days of building of Golden Gate Bridge, some 20 workers died or were seriously injured when they fell into San Francisco Bay. Finally, construction was stopped, and a giant safety net was installed under the work area. Over the next several years, only four men fell off the bridge. Not only did the net make work conditions safer—but it also made workers feel more confident and less likely to fall.

Parents can provide that same security net for their children by making the home a safe place, even when scores tumble. Positive support, rather than faultfinding, increases the likelihood of success in the future. Berating and criticizing a student for poor performance will not make the child work harder, but it will actually create more tension, which can result in even worse grades.

Communicate Grace

Because struggling students sometimes hide hurt behind masks of apathy, the crisis of a poor report card requires extra understanding by parents. When a parent replaces judgment with mercy, however, the child begins to trust parents to help, not hurt.

In offering grace, first remember the guilt and embarrassment your child is already feeling about his poor grades.

Second, separate *who* your child is from the grades he has received. It is no compromise to say, "I know you are disappointed in these marks, but they don't mean you're stupid, and they don't mean I do not love you."

Third, set up a nonthreatening discussion with your child. Go out for ice cream or hot chocolate to discuss his struggles. Look him in the eye and tell him that grades are serious and important, but let him see love—not anger—in your face. Ask your child how you can help him set the course for better grades the next time. Be firm but affectionate. High expectations are good, but grace bends them like a pink eraser to avoid breaking a child's spirit.

Designate a Study Zone

If a child has a routine schedule and a place to do homework, studying will become second nature. The area needs to be quiet and uncluttered. A desk in a bedroom is ideal, but a kitchen table can work, too. Provide good light and keep distractions to a minimum. A dictionary, atlas, and other elementary reference books should be easily accessible, as well as pens, pencils and paper. Consider the child's personal desires as you create a study zone. The goal is to develop the best study conditions for the student, not to force him into a setup he will resist.

Offer to Help

Some parents mistakenly believe that it's the school's job to educate their children. Not at all. You need to augment your child's lessons by taking him to the library, quizzing him on spelling words, reviewing a history chapter, and discussing what he is learning in each class. This makes learning a lifestyle.

But keep in mind that helping is more than an action; it's an attitude. Help doled out as a duty is like a sack lunch without dessert—it may be eaten, but it won't be enjoyed. A spirit of genuine helpfulness allows the struggling student to ask for help without embarrassment.

Energize Your Child's Hope

The old adage "nothing succeeds like success" is not just a cliché. Struggling students need hope. In fact, many educational specialists see hope as the most important ingredient in student success. The child who does not believe he can win in school will sooner or later give up. *I can't do it,* he thinks. *So why try?*

These students need to believe they *can* succeed. You can help insure that your child is in classes that are not over his head. Students who have failed often need success about 90 percent of the time to rebuild their academic confidence. Discuss this goal with your child's teachers to explore the possibilities. With a growing sense of achievement, your child will become more eager to master new material and new skills.

Decrease TV's Magnetic Force

Television can be a roadblock to academic success, since half of all young people spend three or more hours a day in front of its screen. Use it as a reward for completing homework. While it's true that "you can lead a horse to water but you can't make him drink," it's also possible to salt his hay. For some students, a simple reward such as watching television or listening to music is the "salt" that motivates them to study.

In addition, parents have a great deal of moral leverage over their children. The next time you see your child "glued to the tube," sit down and watch with him. Your very presence, even in silence, will instantly make him view the program through different eyes.

If you decide to point out why some programs are destructive, absurd, silly or wasteful, do not preach, "This is bad" or "This is wrong," but offer good reasons for your decisions. The same can be done with rock music or video games. Modeling and quiet reasoning at home will help your child think more skillfully in the classroom.

Listen with an Inner Ear

I worked with school psychologists in dozens of elementary classrooms to help students cope with the aftermath of the Challenger space shuttle disaster. Among our objectives was to teach how emotional jolts influence our capacity to perform effectively.

It doesn't take a national catastrophe to influence your child's ability to concentrate at school. Be sensitive to seemingly small emotional upsets that may impact performance. You may be surprised by the magnitude of the burdens your child feels.

Pay attention, too, to nonverbal behavior (does he avoid eye contact?) and listen to the emotional tone and message behind his words. Even though he says he is "okay," it may mean he is depressed over a classmate's sarcastic comments. Saying, "It sounds as though you had a rough day" can invite a therapeutic dialogue that will clear his thinking so he can begin working hard again. Knowing he is understood at home will help a student perform better in the classroom.

Is the ability to earn good grades inherited or learned? We may never know for sure. But we do know that some students with low grades are crushed by their families while others are rescued by them. A poor report card can be an opportunity to save a child's dignity and clear the way for future improvement.

🌺 🌺 🌺
A Parent's Report Card Checklist

Have you . . .

___ Avoided critical reactions?
___ Expressed love to your child despite his grades?
___ Set up a study zone in your home?
___ Established a daily homework time?
___ Given help to your child when needed?
___ Contacted your child's teacher if necessary?
___ Affirmed your child's potential to succeed in the future?
___ Controlled the use of TV?
___ Used incentives to motivate your child?
___ Expressed your standards firmly but with affection?
___ Sensitively listened to your child's needs and struggles?

_____

Dr. Parrott teaches psychology at Seattle Pacific University.

31

Choosing a College— Already?

Carol Kuykendall

W hat do you want to be when you grow up?"

I remember how that question—usually posed to our young children by a grandmotherly type—flung open the doors to their dreams.

For our eldest child, Derek, the answer depended on the season and his outfit for the day—a fireman, professional football player, or famous basketball player.

For our daughters, Lindsay and Kendall, their fickle answers reflected the current heroine—an ice-skater, television anchorwoman, or veterinarian.

But I remember how that innocent question took on new

243

meaning by their junior year in high school, when teachers, counselors, and even their friends began asking for real.

"Have you given any thought to what you want to do when you grow up?" Derek's counselor asked him as we casually discussed a schedule change.

Derek's eyes widened as he realized it was not a grandmotherly question about childish dreams. He suddenly had no answer at all.

"I just want to be a high school student for now," he moaned.

Kids, like adults, get caught off guard with the realization that the years have passed so quickly, and suddenly it's time to make important decisions.

"Everything starts counting now," we warned our teenagers as they entered high school, but I know we parents walk a tenuous line when we pass along that kind of advice. How do we encourage without pressuring?

I've found that our role as parents is to encourage teens through a series of stressful and confusing choices so they can find a path that seems right for them. In high school, that means determining areas of interest and ability and thinking about options beyond high school.

If college seems to be that option, as it is for nearly 60 percent of all high school graduates, choices become even more important. However, we should assure them that few choices are irreversible. We change our minds; we change classes; we change majors; some people even change schools; and the average American adult changes jobs six times. Many kids are frightened that a choice made in tenth grade may affect them for the rest of their lives.

Even if it's the wrong choice, remind your teen that changes are possible.

In the Maze

The first step through the confusing choices is to take advantage of the resources schools offer. High school counselors have been in the business of helping students through this stage longer than I have as a parent. They offer good materials, including brochures that ask the student some questions to determine interests and strengths: "What are your patterns of choices as they have developed over the years in school, jobs, hobbies, or other activities?" "What's important to you?" "What bugs you?" "How much time do you spend studying?" "Do you enjoy learning?" "What are your most favorite and least favorite subjects in school?"

The Parents' Roles

Here are some things to keep in mind:

• **Give your children a choice.** Instead of predetermining your teen's university, the best things you can do are to gather and give information, identify and state your boundaries or limitations to those choices, and then offer encouragement and support as a choice is made.

We prayed our high school seniors would be accepted by at least two colleges that were acceptable to us, so the final choice would be theirs. At that stage of growing independence, teens need to have ownership of the decision. Otherwise, they won't buy into it with the same sense of personal commitment.

I've known parents who decide that a certain prestigious college is the only right choice, as if acceptance will become an A on their report card of parenting. They don the sweatshirt of that school or proudly place the decal on the back of the family car.

As parents, our goal should be to help our sons and daughters find a school (or other post-high school choice) that's right for *them*. We don't want to set up a situation for failure by pressuring them into choices that aren't right; we want to help them succeed in a college that matches their abilities and prepares them for the vocation they have chosen.

• **Gather and file information.** The amount of information that begins to accumulate regarding college choices and applications quickly overwhelms a high school student. At our house, we felt we might drown in a sea of paper, so we offered to bring order to the chaos, and our students gladly accepted the help.

We first set up a system. My husband, Lynn, is the superorganizer in our family, so he got a sturdy, portable file box with folders and started keeping all the information together, but in separate files.

In addition to keeping track of information, we gathered helpful advice by talking with counselors, teachers and other parents. In fact, parenting a child through this stage of life reminded me of parenting an infant through the baby stage. All that talk about feeding and burping seemed deathly boring and unimportant before we had a baby. Then we had a child, and those conversations suddenly became fascinating. The same is true with conversations about leaving home and choosing colleges. It all seemed so boring a few years ago, but suddenly, we felt magnetically drawn to those conversations as we shared information and encouragement with other parents. "How is the SAT different from the ACT?" we asked each other. "What do you know about John Brown University?" "How do we know if we qualify for financial aid?"

• **Offer advice.** Because we gathered information, we could pass on helpful advice in the areas where our teens were willing to accept it. For instance, we learned that most colleges don't insist on well-rounded students; they prefer well-rounded classes made up of lop-sided students who excel in one or two areas. Most colleges believe that consistently good grades in quality courses are still the best indicators of potential in college; and they especially dislike the choice of "Mickey Mouse" courses during the senior year.

• **Determine and declare limits to the choice.** If we want our students to make the final choice, we need to define our limitations early in the process. For each family, those boundaries will be different. Lynn and I recognized that finding a good college that met the needs of our children for their first year away from home was a high priority and wise investment. We vowed that we would do all we could within our budget to send them to the school that seemed right for them—with a few limitations. We based those limitations on our knowledge of our children—their personalities, strengths, and needs. You may want to actually write out those boundaries. For example: No more than $10,000 a year from *our* pockets; the rest will have to be scholarship money, student loans, etc. No coed dorms. No more than a day's drive from home. No big-city colleges.

• **Consider small schools.** We believe our children need the nurturing, individual attention, and personal challenge found in classes and dormitories at smaller schools, ideally 3,000 students or less. Though some students thrive amidst the stimulation of a large university, we wanted a place where our children were less likely to slip through the cracks, at least for their first year away from home. Both Lynn and I attended large universities where we found ourselves in some classes with 500 other people. Nobody knew if we missed the class; worse, nobody cared. Smaller classes provide an opportunity to know professors personally and to write essay answers to tests (rather than true/false or multiple choice), which teaches students to express themselves and develop their critical-thinking skills.

• **Liberal arts.** Neither of our older children went through high school with a passionate, clear leaning toward a specific career, so we believed a liberal arts college would best prepare them to become competent, knowledgeable, disciplined people who can write and speak effectively, work well with others, and think critically within any chosen field. We believe a liberal arts curriculum educates for life, not just a specific job.

• **Christian or non-Christian.** This is an important consideration, though we didn't make it a strict limitation. For the first year away from home, we believe that a Christian school offers the most nurturing environment and a proper balance between academic excellence and Christian commitment. But we also believe that when it comes to matters of faith, an 18-year-old faces choices, not requirements. We offered our opinions and information, but we didn't limit their choice to a Christian school.

• **Geographical location.** If our teens desired to go away from home or out of state, we encouraged that choice. We believe, if they are ready, that geographical distance increases their potential to gain independence. If they don't make that adjustment to leaving home now, they'll have to make it at some later date.

• **Cost and budget.** Our children know the total budget allotted for their four years of school. Beyond that, they have to share the responsibility of finding financial aid. The fact is, many of the more expensive private institutions offer more financial aid than public institutions.

The Final Decision

Our two older children were accepted by both Christian and non-Christian schools. One seemed clear on a choice; the other struggled a bit more. "How do you know God's will?" one teenager asked.

"If it doesn't seem clear, He may care more about the heart attitude you carry to college than the name of the college," we said.

In the end, one chose a Christian college, while the other chose a non-Christian school. In retrospect (because God's will always seems clearer in hindsight), they both appear to be at the schools that are right for them and on the path of growth divinely designed to meet their needs. Both have felt nurtured by their small-school environments, and both seem challenged. (Admittedly, though, the one attending a non-Christian school faces greater adversity and is forced to answer some tough questions, but that student has also found Christian support within various small groups and is stretching toward great growth.)

As I look back, I'm convinced that students can be happy at several different schools and in many different post-high school experiences. Though the decision is important and profoundly shapes the future of the high school graduate, when we surrender ourselves to God, He weaves all our circumstances together for good.

❈ ❈ ❈

Why choose a Christian school over a non-Christian school?

"If you give me your children for only one year of their lives, give me their freshman year—their first year away from home—when they are most vulnerable and impressionable, bombarded with choices and trying to develop views about life and values and truth and who they are. Let me surround them with some Christian mentors and role models during this tough time of transition."

—a Christian college president

"I strongly believe in Christian education, especially at the collegiate level. . . . The single greatest influence during the college years does not come from the faculty. It is derived from other students! Thus, being classmates with men and women who profess a faith in Jesus Christ is vital to the bonding that should occur during those four years."

—Dr. James Dobson

🌸 🌸 🌸

Student's College-Planning Time Line

Junior Year

February and March: Develop a preliminary list of ten to twelve colleges that sound interesting. Start collecting information from those schools, noting deadlines, tests, and information required for admission. Review your senior-year plan to make sure you are completing all academic courses required by the colleges in which you are interested.

Spring break: Visit college campuses, if possible, noticing the differences between large and small, rural and urban schools. Seek to identify the personalities of each school. Visit classes, eat in the cafeteria, talk with students, and stay in a dormitory.

May: Take advanced placement tests if you qualify. High scorers receive college credits.

Summer: Plan additional campus visits, if possible.

Senior Year

September: Narrow your list of schools to a manageable number—

four to six. Line up teachers to write the recommendations that will accompany your applications. Start thinking about your essays.

November: Take the SAT.

December: Complete and send in applications.

January: Last chance to take the SAT and achievement tests for the fall freshman class. Final deadlines for most applications are between January 15 and March 1. Have your high school counseling office send transcripts of your first semester grades to colleges to which you've applied.

March and April: Acceptance and rejection letters are sent. Continue to do your best work in school; colleges check for signs of senioritis.

Carol Kuykendall lives in Boulder, Colorado, and is the author of *Give Them Wings* published by Focus on the Family.

PART SIX

FOCUS ON FAMILY ACTIVITIES

🌸 32

Stay in Balance

Nancy Thies Marshall

*E*very four years, the world's best athletes compete for Olympic
medals. Like millions around the globe, I'm always glued to
the TV for two weeks of nonstop drama, excitement, and
athletic excellence.

My favorite sport is watching women's gymnastics—my specialty
at the Munich Games in 1972. I was the youngest member of that
U.S. Olympic Team—just a 15-year-old Illinois teen who weighed
100 pounds. I couldn't participate in the opening ceremonies at the
Olympicstade (I had to practice since competition started the next
day), but I can still remember how my stomach churned before the
first event, the uneven bars.

I performed reasonably well, and the team almost won a medal;
we finished fourth. The years certainly haven't dimmed other
Olympic memories: Soviet gymnast Olga Korbut captivating a global
audience with her personality; strolling through the Olympic village,
with its concrete ziggurats and national flags flapping in the breeze;

253

and the horror I felt when Black September terrorists sprang their wave of terror, killing 11 Israeli athletes and coaches.

Fortunately, my parents and four brothers and sisters were in Munich to comfort me. At a young age, I had to come to grips with the realities of an imperfect world.

More than 20 years later, I'm in the midst of a new career as a wife and mother. You could call us a real sports-minded family. My husband, Charlie, played football and baseball at the University of Oregon, and our children, Ryan, seven, and Caitlin, three, love their gymnastics lessons. In the last year, Ryan has also played in organized soccer and T-ball leagues, coached by his dad!

Often, when I'm driving the kids to another practice, I wonder if Charlie and I will be able to raise them with the right attitudes about sports and competition. *How can we keep the fun in sports without going overboard on winning and losing? If one of our children becomes a standout athlete, how can we nurture that talent without ignoring the needs of the other child? How can sports bolster their faith in Christ?*

These are important questions, ones often asked by parents whose children are heavily involved in swimming, soccer, gymnastics, baseball, basketball, football, tennis, or taekwondo, to name a few. If sports play a big part in your family, here are several ideas to keep in mind:

• *Encourage the development of godly character.* I remember my dad saying, "Mom and I have supported you in gymnastics, not because you won meets or came home with trophies, but because your character has been strengthened by the challenges you faced."

During my rise in the world of gymnastics, my parents kept me on an even keel by occasionally placing Bible verses on humility next to my corn flakes. When I did poorly—usually on those uneven bars—they still reminded me of God's promise that "in all things God works for the good of those who love him" (Rom. 8:28).

• *Don't let sports become more important than church.* My parents always helped me make time to develop my relationship with the Lord. Not only did they accompany me to church, but they prodded

me to take part in youth group activities. I see now that it was important to make friends with peers outside the gym.

- *Keep schoolwork a priority.* Schoolwork not only balances the
rigors of athletics and broadens a child's perspective, but it's also more
important in the long run. One year, I was struggling with my history
class. My parents and coach agreed I could take a week off from practice to study. That was a nice reminder that school was a top priority.

The fall was always a time when I could back off gymnastics a bit
and concentrate on my studies. I also established a rapport with my
teachers, so when the busy spring season arrived, they were flexible
with my travel schedule. They knew I wasn't going to let my schoolwork falter.

If you're a parent of an exceptional athlete, he or she will have to
take some time off from school every now and then.

I remember one night just before the 1972 Olympic Trials, my
father drove me home at 11:00 P.M. following an important meet. He
told me I could sleep in the next day and miss school. I could do that
because I had kept up with my schoolwork.

- *Be sure to have an "off-season."* Sports psychologists agree that
athletes who keep the pressures of competition in balance are those
who have purposely scheduled "downtime" in their training. Our
children need some time off, too—a period to goof off and have fun
away from their sport.

- *Watch out for sibling rivalry.* My parents were always on the
lookout for signs of discord. Dinnertime conversation didn't center
around my workouts and upcoming meets, but rather on current
events, church activities, and upcoming plans.

Every so often, my parents organized "sing-along" nights, and one
of my sisters played the piano while a brother strummed the guitar. We
gathered around and sang hymns and folk songs. This strengthened
family ties, and it was amazing how our sibling rivalries melted away.

- *Continue family traditions.* The most significant thing we did as
a family was our annual summer vacation at a Wisconsin lake cot-
tage. We used the time to talk about goals for the next year and

renew our walk with the Lord, as Dad often led family worship. I've found that when you're away from the normal routine, the opportunities for communication are a lot better. I'm convinced those vacations helped keep our family on track.

• *Establish a good relationship with the coach.* If your child is on a team, it's important that you support the coach. Let him or her know that you appreciate the time invested into your child. Ask how you can help.

We have "team parents" in Ryan's T-ball league who telephone other moms and dads about upcoming games and arrange who's going to bring the post-game drinks.

Can you volunteer in other ways? Can you referee a soccer sideline, move gym equipment, drive to out-of-town meets, help with the clean up or host year-end parties? This support goes a long way to provide an encouraging environment for your child.

• *Realize the odds of your son or daughter going to the Olympics or playing a professional sport are infinitesimal.* Some parents see their child excel at the local level, and all of a sudden the pressure is on. Visions of million-dollar contracts and huge endorsement fees dance around their heads.

Well, Dad, the chances of your son becoming the next Barry Bonds aren't much better than my making the Olympic team again. In gymnastics alone, there are 38,000 girls competing in sanctioned meets this year. Only *six* will make the U.S. Olympic team!

Goals are good, but it's even more important to see your child's involvement in sports as part of a broader picture. My parents believed gymnastics could help me mature and become a responsible adult. Any successes I enjoyed on the mat were a bonus.

• *Don't be a pushy "sports mom" or "sports dad."* We've all seen them—the dad with the bullhorn voice who constantly rides the referee; the mom who's always complaining to sports administrators. Kids see that, too. An obnoxious parent will kill a child's enthusiasm. I've seen more talented children lose their drive because a parent pushed too much.

A delicate balance is needed. As a parent, I don't want to relinquish my responsibilities. Many professional coaches are not experts in child rearing and don't see that as part of their job description. They are paid to get the most out of their athletes, and unless parents keep a close eye on the situation, many children can get chewed up in the process.

But you also have to know *when* to loosen the reins so you don't smother any progress your child is making. My parents communicated their respect for my coach's authority by letting *him* do the coaching, but they made it clear that parental authority rested with them.

• *Support your child, win or lose.* What do you say when your child loses? Not much. Sympathize with him. Your child is probably hurting. A lot of parents mumble, "Better luck next time," but I think it's more important for a mom or dad to say, "I'm sorry you lost. I hurt with you. Tell me what you're feeling."

When you're having your discussion, don't talk *at* him, but *with* him. Point out the things he did that you're proud of. Discourage your child from making excuses. Simply look at how he could have done better. When it's appropriate, ask, "What did you learn from this?"

• *View unfair results as character-building opportunities.* In 1971, when I was 14, I qualified for my first international competition in Europe. I was on cloud nine! But the coach replaced me with a lower-ranked gymnast.

I remember standing in our kitchen crying my eyes out. My father hugged me and said, "Nancy, welcome to the real world, a world where life is not always fair." When the tears finally stopped, my parents reminded me that my bigger goal was to make the Olympic team. I used that incident to work even harder in the gym.

• *Pray with your child for God's best.* Don't pray to win. After all, if others are whispering the same prayer, what will the Lord do? I remember the final event at the '72 Olympic Trials. I was tied for sixth place, and only six would compete in Munich.

I went behind the bleachers and prayed, "Lord, help me to do my best." Since I had no control over my score, that really took the pressure off. I simply had to try my hardest. I went out there and performed well in the floor exercise, clinching a berth on the U.S. Olympic team.

As I matured in Christ, my prayers included a gratefulness for the opportunity to perform. Praying to demonstrate a Christlike attitude before others also gave me a broader purpose for my endeavors.

• *What do you say when the child wins?* Make sure your child understands the correlation between hard work and victory. Help him be humble. Constantly remind him of the Scripture, "For everyone who exalts himself will be humbled, and he who humbles himself will be exalted" (Luke 14:11).

• *Encourage excellence while loving your child unconditionally.* I'll never forget the time Dad took me aside just before the '74 World Championship trials. "We want you to know that whatever happens in the future, we are proud of you. Your performance has nothing to do with our estimation of you." In Mom and Dad's eyes, high or low marks didn't determine my worth.

These days, I often help out at the local gym. I've seen parents give their child a cold shoulder or a verbal beating after a poor performance. Yet a simple hug and a warm smile can set the stage for a more fruitful conversation later on about what went wrong. Remember to love your child unconditionally, as Christ loves us.

In that context, the pressures of our success-oriented world will lessen as we encourage our children to strike a healthy balance in their pursuit of God's best.

Following the 1972 Olympics, Nancy competed in the Soviet Union, Bulgaria, and South Africa. After graduating from the University of Illinois, she became a gymnastics commentator for NBC Sports and a seminar speaker. The Marshalls live in Salem, Oregon.

🌿 33

Drawing a Family Circle

Cheri Fuller

*A*unts and uncles, first, second and third cousins, sit together and enjoy each other's company in Lonny and Beverly Borts' living room in Syosset, New York. Reminiscing, laughter, and lots of news are being swapped—a recent graduation, two weddings, and the birth of a seventh-generation baby. Photographs of cousins in New Zealand are passed around.

This is no ordinary Saturday night party; it's the Littman Family Circle gathering, which meets five times a year. From its earliest beginnings in 1936, the Littman Family Circle has "strengthened the ties that bind us together as relatives and friends," says its president, Marilyn Brenner of Teaneck, New Jersey.

The Littman Family Circle has kept the family in contact through picnics, anniversary dinners, a regular newsletter, and even a book of family history and genealogy written by Mrs. Brenner.

Besides meeting socially and sharing news, Family Circle members also help each other out: writing letters of recommendation for a son's first job, rounding up volunteers to visit a great aunt in a nursing home, and collecting money for a "Sunshine Fund" to help a family in need.

From Young to Old

In upstate New York, the Podolny Family Circle has members whose ages range from 10 months to 86 years. "Our Family circle brings a great feeling of belonging, closeness, and family unity," says Blanche Liebman of Hartsdale, New York. "Because everyone lives fairly close to each other, we meet every month. When my husband had bypass surgery, family members called and visited. The also sent us gifts."

How did family clubs get their start? "Many immigrants came to this country between 1881 and 1914—as my grandfather did—and they all lived close to one another," explains Rabbi David Packman of Temple B'nai Israel in Oklahoma City. "But the grandchildren of immigrants left for the nearby affluent neighborhoods. Then with the spreading of this generation across the country came a desire to keep in touch through Cousins' Clubs and Family Circles. They've been very successful."

As a child growing up in Philadelphia, Rabbi Packman attended his mother's Cousins' Club monthly gatherings. "We had Sunday brunch in an aunt's or uncle's home and then stayed to visit through the afternoon and evening. By then, you were filled in on everyone's news. If a relative was sick, money was collected. If a need for child care or personal help arose, someone volunteered," says the rabbi.

In today's get-up-and-go society, the splintering of the family has not gone unnoticed. "I think what is happening is that the family has gone from something people took for granted or found burdensome to something that is like sand slipping though your fingers," said Ira Wolfman, author of *The Kids' Book of Genealogy: A Guide for Ancestor Detectors*. "If you don't hold on to what you've got, you suddenly discover that it's gone."

Family Circles were the backdrop to a 1991 Hollywood movie, "Avalon," the story of a Jewish immigrant from Poland, Sam Kachinsky. "I came to America in 1914," he tells his grandchildren often. "It was the most beautiful place I'd ever seen."

As "Avalon" demonstrated, many Family Circles fell by the way-side following World War II. "I thought it would be interesting to show the evolution of a family over a five-year period—how the structure changes and the extended family disappears," said writer/director Barry Levinson. "I grew up with my grandparents and parents, and aunts and uncles came through the house all the time. We had a real sense of family; but now that's part of vanishing America."

Bringing back Family Circles—even if members live thousands of miles away—is one way to stem the tide. "One of the great benefits is regaining the continuity people are lacking," says Tully Plesser, part of the Schreiber Family Circle, which has members far and wide: Los Angeles, Toronto, New York, Florida, Israel, and Europe. "Children develop a sense of belonging. They realize they have ties to different sizes, shapes, and kinds of people, not just their little family unit."

As a child, Plesser was inspired by the different qualities and achievements of relatives he met in Family Circle gatherings—a concert pianist, an author, a physician, among others. "I was exposed to excellent role models," he said, "and achievement became more attainable because these people were close to home. It motivated me to say, 'People from my family can do that, and so can I!' "

Making the Move

Anytime is a good time to start a Family Circle. Here are some tips:
- **Make the first step.** You can be the catalyst for your family to grow closer. Gather names and addresses of family members living near you and choose a time to meet. Send out invitations and a short letter explaining why you want to start a Family Circle. Even if only three or four people show up, your circle will grow. *You have to start somewhere!*

If you're isolated from other relatives, you might schedule a Family Circle meeting at a family wedding. Remember, it's too hectic to meet *before* the wedding; shoot for the day after, usually a Sunday.

"Don't be too structured at first, locking people in too tightly," says Tully Plesser. "Being flexible and keeping ground rules to a minimum helps people feel more comfortable."

• **Divide up responsibilities.** One family can volunteer to have the next gathering at their home. Another committee can bring food and refreshments. Several couples can help gather names and addresses for the roster, an important part of the Family Circle.

"If you're traveling, the family roster is invaluable for making connections," says Ira Wolfman. "If we're going to San Diego, for example, we look in our directory to see if we have distant cousins there. Then we give them a call and get together."

Ricki Schreiber of Los Angeles uses a computer spread sheet to gather information for her Family Circle roster. Each person receives a blank form asking for name, address, phone, birthday, anniversary, and names and birth dates of children. There's also room to report family news, achievements, weddings, and other happenings, which are compiled for the cover letter sent each year with the roster.

The Schreiber mailing is paid through volunteer dues that have other uses as well. In the Schreiber family, members contribute twice a year to an emergency fund that provides clothing, holiday food, and medical expenses for relatives in need. A portion is also earmarked for charities.

• **Make sure you have fun, too.** At your first meeting, plan a social time to visit and swap news. Says Ann Davis of Lake Worth, Florida, "I think you'll find as you're sitting close to each other, much is shared. Gatherings generate a lot of warmth and spontaneity. In the Family Circle, relationships have a head start."

At Ann's "Cousins' Club" gatherings, relatives fill in missing pieces of the puzzle of family history. With the different impressions and stories coming from sisters and cousins about their parents and grandparents, they all learn a lot about their heritage.

Taping oral histories at gatherings is a great way to value both the older people in the family and the history. "Taping is a wonderful thing to do," says author Ira Wolfman. "It affects people deeply and teaches you about your own origins."

Some Family Circle gatherings include an informal business meeting to plan a future reunion, make announcements, or discuss needs with the group. Others include a simple worship service.

Some gatherings are just for fun—a picnic, a camping trip, or an outing. The Littman Family Circle is planning to meet at Ellis Island this summer to retrace their ancestors' steps.

• **A newsletter is essential.** Distance is a problem for many families, but a report such as *The Littman Log* or *The Jordan Journal* is a wonderful tool to keep everyone in touch. "The newsletter is a major factor in helping families stay connected," says Tully Plesser.

A newsletter can be handwritten, typed and copied, or computer-generated, and should include everything from news of the family to anecdotes from the past. Some even include copies of old documents discovered in an attic.

You can also share information about births, graduations, and military service in a "General Family News" section. Some families list birthdays and anniversaries for the next few months (so members can send greetings). You might also announce the next get-together, or have one family member describe a recent trip to China or what it's like to be stationed in a foreign country.

• **Share your faith.** Being in a Family Circle is also a great way to share your faith and provides many opportunities for ministry. What can be more rewarding than bringing a family member into the Kingdom!

34

Pizza for Breakfast?

Dean Merrill

*I*t's 7:45 A.M., and Denise Christian's first-hour Spanish class in a suburban Chicago high school is reviewing food terms. *Queso* (cheese). *Huevos* (eggs). *Frijoles refritos* (refried beans). *Arroz con pollo* (chicken with rice).

"Suddenly I realize a couple of my students aren't tracking," says Christian, a nine-year veteran of teaching. "The one turns to the other and says, 'Man, I'm starving.' Like many teenagers today, he has shown up at school without breakfast.

"His friend has a solution. 'Hey, why didn't you grab a piece of cold pizza like I did? It works great.' "

Welcome to nutrition in the '90s. So much for antiques like oatmeal or grapefruit.

Family mealtimes in North America are on a skid, according to nearly every new poll. Three-fourths of families now eat together only half the time. Some of these separations are necessary, of course, due to work and school. But a lot more are lifestyle choices: sitting down in the kitchen can't compete with working out at the gym, staying late at the office, or simply not wanting to wait on someone else.

"Probably half this community works downtown," says Denise Christian, "which means dads—and moms—are up very early to catch the train or hit the expressway. Kids get themselves off to school. Our cafeteria opens shortly after 7:00, and while you won't find eggs or pancakes, at least bagels, fruit, cold cereal, and milk are available."

The biggest seller?

"Doughnuts," replies Denise.

That means some students are already on a sugar high before the first bell rings. Denise, in fact, looks out at a sharp contrast: "The hyper kids who've been to the cafeteria, and the sluggish kids who haven't eaten a thing and are still waking up. It's one or the other." And people wonder why teaching is such hard work these days.

Why We "Don't Bother" Anymore

So far as I know, nobody *decided* over the last 30 years to slack off on eating together as families. It just sort of happened, due to a number of factors. Employment is certainly one. It takes longer to get to and from work in today's traffic, and modern bosses want more time once we're there.

The steady rise in the number of employed *women*—she traditional cooks in most families—has had its effect. Wives' time and energy for fussing in the kitchen is greatly curtailed; simply getting the weekly *shopping* done is an achievement.

Meanwhile, modern technology—most notably the microwave—has made every family member his own cook . . . sort of. When each person can pop in a Ravioli Lunch Bucket or a Lean Cuisine, why "bother" trying to eat together?

In fact, things go smoother if you *don't*; microwaves are one-at-a-time machines, so wait your turn. Hopefully, you'll find some fresh lettuce or an apple in the fridge to fill in missing nutrients.

If zap-cooking takes too much effort, a battery of fast-food chains waits at every stoplight—another invention of the late-20th century. Speedy and cheap (but it adds up), propelled by razzle-dazzle advertising, they provide exactly what millions are looking for. The notion of roast beef, mashed potatoes, or even five-cup fruit salad grows dimmer by the month.

So does the notion of actually *talking* to each other over a plate of food. Hearing what went well—or badly—during the day. Enjoying a joke together. Debating an issue. Looking forward to a challenge—a report to give at school, an important sales call, a special song to perform at church.

To one busy, breathless parent, Dr. Dobson wrote the following comments: "It takes time to be an effective parent. . . . It takes time to listen, once more, to the skinned-knee episode and talk about the bird with a broken wing. These are the building blocks of esteem, held together with the mortar of love. But they seldom materialize amidst busy timetables. . . .

"The great value of traditions is that they give a family a sense of identity and belonging. All of us desperately need to feel that we're not just part of a busy cluster of people living together in a house, but we're a living breathing family that's conscious of our uniqueness, our character, and our heritage."

In Defense of "Bothering"

I didn't realize how much cultural shift had taken place until a recent evening, when our two teenage daughters reported, "Our friends at school think we're totally weird that we eat breakfast and dinner together as a family. They're just astounded—like, 'You must be the Waltons or something.'"

I got the feeling *weird* was actually more of a compliment (in a weird sort of way). My wife and I haven't always felt like adjusting our schedules to accommodate a family mealtime, but over the years we've come to believe it's worth the effort. Our current weekly count stands at fourteen out of fifteen. (We miss lunches Monday through Friday, plus Saturday breakfast—teenagers sleep in, remember?)

Sure, it means getting up earlier than we would otherwise have to. Sure, it means leaving the office when work is still crying to be done—actually, packing it in a briefcase for later in the evening. But over the past 25 years at our house, the rhythm of regular family meals has proven its worth.

Granted, some parents do have to work odd shifts. A friend of mine supervises a grocery distribution depot and has to be on the job at 4:00 A.M.—I doubt his clan would appreciate being awakened for family breakfast together! But special cases aside, most of us could increase our weekly count with some minor adjusting, if we truly wanted to. Here are four reasons to think about it:

• *Overall nutrition.* The easiest things to pop in our mouths are not always the best. High-fat, high-starch diets are having an undeniable effect on this society. The Harvard Nutrition and Fitness Project says child obesity is up 54 percent since the 1960s.

(Is it true, or is it just my imagination that people who skip breakfast are more prone to overcompensating later in the day—and thus more prone to weight problems? Children, of course, do whatever they see adults doing. Anyway . . .)

"When I examine five-year-olds getting ready for kindergarten," says Dr. Jerry Hough, a Florida pediatrician, "I give the mom a little speech. I say, 'Look, I've checked for anemia and a dozen other problems, you've invested in all the shots—now do one more thing. Get this child off to school with a good breakfast.' "

To a mom who says there just isn't time, or she doesn't like breakfast herself, Dr. Hough says: "Well, stir up an instant-breakfast drink for yourself and your child; at least you'll get 250 calories that way."

Dr. Hough, like most physicians, discourages arguing with a child over food *choice:* "Don't have World War III at the table. But at least provide the healthy things. If you're not sure what that entails, ask your doctor or a nutritionist."

Probably the smartest trick is to not allow snacking *between* meals, so the child comes to the table hungry. "Food battles are far less frequent then."

On the other end of the spectrum, some kids—especially teen girls—don't want to eat at all. They can get away with it in a family without regular mealtimes. Who's to notice an incipient anorexic if nobody's in the kitchen at the same time?

• *School performance*. My wife, who has taught third grade in a Los Angeles-area Christian school, says she could tell within seconds which students return from morning recess having dug a candy bar out of their lunch bags or backpacks. Sugar and reading groups just don't work well together.

Even educators in traditional, rural areas are facing new headaches. Darlene Gates is now in her 17th year of teaching in Sully, Iowa, population 800—the heartland of America. Cornfields and hog farms cover the rolling hills in every direction; the nearest city is more than an hour away.

"Every year or so I ask my fifth-graders, 'How many of you had toast or milk or juice this morning?' Never do I get more than half the hands in the room. And these are the sons and daughters of people who *grow* the breakfast foods for the rest of the nation!"

Mrs. Gates then asks her students what they ate before they came to school. The answers are things like "Oh, a can of pop" or "Nothing."

• *Communication*. Ever notice how much time Jesus spent talking with people *over meals*? Lazarus, Mary, and Martha . . . Simon the Pharisee . . . Zacchaeus . . . the Twelve on Passover Night. He knew that people relax more then, that their minds sort of open along with their mouths, and that special closeness can develop.

In tragic contrast, think about the modern child eating alone. Where does he plop down with his bowl of Golden Grahams? In front of the TV. He's silently pleading for communication.

That's why mealtime talk must relate to kids as well as adults; long discussions of job tensions or the family budget are best handled elsewhere. This is a time to be one another's *friends*. Best-selling author

Stephen Covey's principle of "Seek first to understand, then to be understood" is a good one here. It's time to ask can-opener questions like "Who had something terrific happen today?" or "How did you feel about that?" or "Let's talk about this coming weekend. What would be fun to do?"

What if the talk turns negative, sarcastic, or complaining? Parents must not let the atmosphere be sabotaged. When our kids were younger, I was known to deal with bickering by silently picking up a child's plate, cup, and silverware—and transporting them to the top of the washing machine! The child had temporarily lost his or her right to enjoy the family table. And *standing up* for the rest of the meal while looking at nothing but a lonely Maytag was a strong message that pleasant talk would be the wiser route next time.

We've also set a firm policy on menu comments: *If you can't say something good, don't say anything.* The parent who *didn't* do the cooking is the better one to enforce this.

Erma Bombeck once spoke for every frustrated mom when she cracked, "Why should I take pride in cooking when they don't take pride in eating?" The "eaters" have a responsibility to honor the effort of the "cooker."

• *Most important of all, the "Somebody loves me" message.* Regular, reliable meals, whether fancy or simple, send a quiet message to any child that *Someone is planning for me. Someone cares about my daily needs. Someone is regularly thinking of my good.*

Yes, it's a bother sometimes. Yes, it means bending our schedules. But isn't that our calling as dads and moms? "After all," wrote the apostle Paul, "children should not have to provide for their parents, but parents should provide for their children" (2 Cor. 12:14, GNB).

While all of us in the 1990s face particular stresses, we must not forever yield to circumstances. Our children deserve the simple gift of daily bread they can count on. And as we give it, we find a special joy coming back our way that frantic, splintered households will never know.

❈ ❈ ❈
Recipe for Better Mealtimes

1. Plan ahead. Start early enough. Have the right food on hand.
2. Insist on prompt attendance when called. Don't allow a come-when-you-feel-like-it habit.
3. Turn off the TV.
4. Turn off the radio. (The point is to listen to *each other*, not the weatherman or disc jockey!)
5. Start with a table prayer, genuinely expressed. Call on a different family member to lead each time. But keep it short.
6. Keep the atmosphere positive. Don't allow "attacks" on the food quality or one another.
7. Don't fight over quantities, expecially with preschoolers, who often go on feast-or-famine jags. Hunger will prevail over time. However, if for social reasons you want to require that children "try some of everything on the table," fine.
8. Involve everyone in the conversation.

Dean Merrill is vice president of publications at Focus on the Family.

35

Daddy's Home

Greg Johnson and Mike Yorkey

No warship in the world is larger than the *USS Nimitz*, a nuclear-powered aircraft carrier. The *Nimitz* stretches 1,092 feet long and has nearly five acres of flight deck. Yet this 100,846-ton "flattop" can zip along in excess of 30 knots, and she can travel a million miles without refueling.

Today's families are much like aircraft carriers. We often get headed in one direction—and it's hard to change course. Other times, the storms of life buffet our boat, but we usually ride it out.

Like the *Nimitz*'s abundance of technology and hardware, family life is getting more and more complicated as we steam toward the year 2000. Families need constant attention and maintenance these days, but we also need "downtime" to recharge our batteries.

The captain of the family is the father. At least, that's been God's design all along. A father's duties include loving his wife and children, providing strong leadership, earning a living to support the family, and imparting spiritual values to his kids. And that's just the short list.

We interviewed dozens of fathers, and usually our first question was: "So, what makes a good dad?" Invariably, nearly all the dads stressed the importance of spending *time* with their children.

Of course, that's the no-brainer answer we expected—and *wanted*—to hear from fathers who are getting the job done. The importance of spending time with children is a truism that needs to be repeated as much as possible. Why? Because time is a non-renewable resource; once it's gone, it's gone.

Four Words You'll Never Want to Say

Roy, a Midwestern professional, recalls a job that required a lot of out-of-state travel. "The first 10 to 12 years after the kids were born, my work took me away quite a bit," he says. "My wife was really good about it, and she did a great job of raising our three kids. When they hit early adolescence, however, it suddenly dawned on me that I had missed out on a great deal. After much reflection, I did something I never thought I could do: I quit that high-paying job. Then I went out and found a new job that would keep me close to home. But despite all I did, it was too late," he laments.

"No matter how hard I tried to put myself back into my kids' lives, it didn't work. They had adjusted to the point where having Dad around wasn't necessary. Now, seven years later, we're a little happier, but it's not anything like I wish it could be. I missed my chance, and *now it's too late*."

That's right, Dad. If you're not around, your wife and children will learn to live life without you. It's as if you're the manager of the New York Yankees, but you don't arrive at the ballpark until the seventh inning. You'll find the players and coaches playing the game without you. Life goes on.

Not every dad who feels he must pour his best years into his work (or has a job that forces him to travel) will end up with a lifetime of regret. But since we're given only a short time with our children, the best years to get them on our team are when they're young.

Some Ideas

If you agree that spending time with kids is a great idea—right up there with ordering a hot dog at a ball game—how *can* you do it? Here are some ideas the fathers we interviewed shared with us:

• *If possible, rearrange your work schedule.* Herb is an orthopedic surgeon in Akron, Ohio. At 43, he is getting his practice established, but Herb knows the medical profession can gobble up hours in huge chunks.

"How do I spend time with my kids?" said Herb, repeating the question. "I'm not a morning person, so I've changed my hours around. That way, I don't have to go into the office right away. I can eat breakfast with my kids and take them to school. I'll start my surgeries at one o'clock in the afternoon and go until 7:00 P.M. or so."

• *Make dinner a priority.* Dinner is a time to reconnect. There's something about the entire family sitting around and enjoying a meal together. And in this day and age of working moms, long commutes, and kids in sports, it's no easy chore for everyone to sit down together.

Eating together promotes communication, which promotes discussion, which promotes sharing, which promotes love. Did you ever notice that when you eat alone you flip on the TV? You want some sort of communication, even if it's one-way.

Dinnertime together is also a great way to know what's going on in your kids' lives. Brad, a New England father, says when the family sits down at the table, he asks each child, "What was the best thing that happened to you today?"

"Doing that stimulates talk, and everyone has to listen," says Brad. "That way, we begin the dinner conversation with a positive focus, and I try to remember something each one said so when it's time for nightly prayer, I can say, 'Thanks, Lord, for helping Jeremy pass the test.' "

In the last year, Brad has tried to spend some *unscheduled* time with his kids, too. Sometimes he'll knock on the bedroom door and ask to come in and just talk. "It's amazing how kids will open up then," he says.

- *Ban the TV*. What story worth its salt wouldn't suggest this? But letting the hours vaporize into thin air because the "boob tube" drones on and on *is* a waste of time. Apparently, the fathers we interviewed agreed. Nearly one-third (29 percent) said they don't watch any TV during the week, and 61 percent said they watch one to two hours a night—a manageable figure. So, nine out of ten dads have the TV under control.

- *Do "Daddy Dates."* Westy, a Wisconsin father, says he can think of nothing better than taking his nine-year-old daughter out for breakfast or dinner. "She knows the only reason we're going out is so we can talk," says Westy. "We probably get as much conversation in during that one meal as we do all week. We sit across the table from each other and converse; there's a lot of questions and answers going on. These 'Daddy Dates' tell my daughter that she is very, very important to me."

A good time to start "dating" your child is around eight or nine years old. "Don't wait until he or she is fifteen years old. That's too late," says Westy. By spending individual time with your child, you build a friendship, so when the *really* big discussions pop up later (love, dating, and sex), a foundation has already been laid.

- *Include your children in your vacations*. You'd be surprised at the number of families who vacation *without* their kids. When Randy, a Texas rancher, and his family go on vacation, they drive. That way, Randy's certain they'll have plenty of time in the car. (Believe it or not, that's the way he wants it!) One of the kids sits with Dad in the front seat, and as the scenery passes by, long discussions ensue.

- *Volunteer to coach your child's sports team*. When you make that commitment to coach, it *forces* you to spend time with your children. That's the way Jeffrey, a Sacramento father, slices out hours with his four children (ranging in age from three to 15). He's coached baseball for eight years, from Little League through Pony League.

"Baseball is a real competitive sport here in California, and with a lot of competition comes a lot of pressure. There's a struggle in keeping sports in the right perspective. I tell my boys to use the talents the

Lord gives them—but to have fun, too. I think the lessons sports teach are good for kids because they learn about life's ups and downs," says Jeffrey.

- *If you can't be a coach, then cheer from the grandstands.* Max, an attorney, said he always wanted to take time to be with Max Jr. while he was growing up, but he (Max Sr.) wasn't the athletic type.

"I didn't coach, but I went to all the Little League games, where I could encourage him. And when he started playing high school football, I was there, even for his J.V. games that started at 3:00 P.M. I was lucky to have a job with flexible hours."

Max adds that he and his wife had made an early commitment to go to *everything* at school—recitals, sports, band concerts, you name it. "Even if the kids tell you they don't want you to show up, they really do," says the Windy City dad.

- *Make the best use of your recreational time.* It's important to exercise our bodies (we feel better when we're in good shape). Many of us enjoy the spirit of competition. Some recreational pursuits, however, take up a lot of time.

Take golf, for instance. As Baby Boomers age, golf is *the* sport of the '90s. Yet when I (Mike) play, it burns up most of a Saturday. Even if I'm a member of the "dawn patrol," I'm still not home till noon. I've decided golf is going to have to wait.

That's why I play a lot of tennis, but I've had to cut back there, too. Usually, I'll play one or two mornings a week *before* work, starting at 6:15 A.M. I figure it's better to play while the kids are still sleeping than to practice my forehand after work when they're home.

- *Finally, remember that your kids are keeping tabs on you.* When 1,500 schoolchildren were asked by social scientists John DeFrain and Nick Stinnett, "What do you think makes a happy family?", the children didn't list money, fine homes, or big-screen TVs. No, the answer most frequently offered was "doing things together."

"I once saw a sign in the nursery," said Herb, the orthopedic surgeon. "It said: 'Children spell love T-I-M-E.' You can't buy your kids' affection unless you spend your time with them."

✣ ✣ ✣

Where's Your Time Going?

Out of a 168-hour week, American men on the average devoted 56 hours to work, 70 hours to sleeping, eating, and personal care, and 42 hours to leisure activities.

So, let's do a little exercise: Grab a pencil and determine how you "spent" your last 24 hours (make it a weekday):

- Sleeping_____
- Grooming_____
- Working (main job) _____
- Commuting_____
- Overtime or moonlighting_____
- Household chores_____
- Eating with the family_____
- Leisure pursuits (exercise, reading, hobbies) _____

After you've added up the hours, ask yourself these questions:

- Was this a routine day?
- How much time did I spend with my children?
- What did I do with them?
- Was I home for dinner?
- Did I do paperwork while Mom bathed the kids and put them down?
- Did I talk with my wife?
- How much time was frittered away watching TV?

✣ ✣ ✣

Some of the Worst Ways to Spend Time with Your Kids

1. Serve as their human quarter machine at the video arcade.
2. Have the NBA playoff game on while you're playing Monopoly with them.

3. Read the paper while helping them with their algebra assignments.
4. Go to the local high school football field to practice your short-
   irons, and have them collect the golf balls after you're done.
5. Suggest they take a nap with you on a beautiful Sunday afternoon.
6. Drive them to Cub Scouts and read a magazine in the car while
   the den mother instructs them on how to tie knots.
7. Take them to your office on Saturday and have them color while
   you work.

Greg Johnson is a literary agent for Alive Communications in Colorado Springs.
Mike Yorkey is editor of *Focus on the Family* magazine. This article is adapted from *Daddy's Home*, published by Tyndale Publishers, copyright © 1992 by Greg Johnson and Mike Yorkey, and is used by permission of the publisher.

36

The Joy of Camping

Bob Welch

The clouds above Suttle Lake in Oregon's Cascade mountains were thick and black, like smoke from burning tires. When you're 10 years old and think camping is the coolest thing since the invention of Fizzies, you don't want to see a sky like that, particularly on the day your family vacation has begun.

So you wait and listen and hope, and then you hear those reassuring words.

"Ah, it's just a squall," said my dad, looking at the charcoal sky. "It'll pass in no time."

My guess is it passed sometime shortly before my high school graduation. Our family—Mom, Dad, and my older sister—spent that entire weekend sitting under a tarp, listening to the rain fill the plastic and spill to the ground. We told every knock-knock joke we'd ever heard. We not only read every article in the two dog-eared

281

Reader's Digests we'd brought, but the magazine's staff box and Statement of Ownership as well.

But I wouldn't trade that memory for anything.

From Father to Son

I thought about that vacation not long ago while camping with my wife and two boys, the oldest of whom is 10. Some families, I realized, are linked by a recreational pursuit passed down from generation to generation. For our family, it's camping.

Like my parents before me and my father's parents before him, we are woven together by some inexplicable desire to get smoke in our eyes, sit on fishing lures, and offer ourselves as human sacrifices to tribes of blood-thirsty mosquitoes.

Why? It's easy to answer when you're watching a full moon reflect on a high mountain lake, or observing a chipmunk steal M&Ms, or reading Psalms as the wind tickles the branches of the Douglas firs. It's tougher to answer when it's 5:00 A.M., and you're the only one in the tent not sleeping, a tree root poking between your shoulder blades. Or when some guy three campsites away is snoring as if he were a chainsaw with a worn-out carburetor.

When my oldest son was four years old, we had been fishing for days in a small boat when he suddenly said, "Dad, why do we fish?"

He was not concerned about the ethics of the sport. He was perplexed because he had never seen me catch a fish. He didn't understand the object of our mission. You sat in a boat the size of a bathtub and threw worms on hooks over the side. You talked in whispers while your cramped legs went to sleep. What sort of strange ritual was this?

Now that I've grown up, I find myself pondering the same question. Why give up microwave ovens and soft mattresses for eight-foot boats and outhouses that are too far away when you need one and too close when you don't?

Part of the reason we camp and fish, I think, is because of that heartfelt utterance of Tevye in *Fiddler on the Roof*: Tradition! Ours is a world where traditions are easily trampled. So we parents want our children to have the experiences we had as a child.

Thus, we go camping—and bring the flashlight whose batteries have been dead since the Reagan administration. We forget the can opener, so we mutilate a can of Dinty Moore beef stew with a knife. And we use nearly as much blood, sweat, and tears putting up a 12-foot nylon tent as the Egyptians used in building the pyramids.

Singing Along

Take camp songs for example. As a boy, I remember groaning when my mother broke into songs while we sat around the fire, including one about how we "love to go a-wandering. . . ." Now I'm the one who breaks into songs as my children sing in sweet harmony. It's traditional.

Take marshmallows. They make no particular sense. They're full of sugar. Within seconds over a hot fire, they become charred torches with the epicurean appeal of coal. And the mushy part inside usually winds up in a child's hair, attracts a weekend's worth of pine needles and ultimately has to be clear-cut with a pair of scissors. But you must roast marshmallows while camping. It's traditional.

Why else do we camp? Because it brings us face to face, not only as tent sardines, but as human beings. At home, too often we gather around the TV, each of us reacting to the tube, not to each other. High in the mountains, we gather around a fire, which draws us to each other.

Never mind that the same fire, before the weekend is out, will melt the toe of at least one child's tennis shoe and spew ashes into someone's hot chocolate. Camp fires stir memories, prompt small talk, and, as the evening deepens and the embers glow more faintly, nudge us into bigger talk.

We might start the evening laughing about a squirrel on the cooler and wind up talking about the Sermon on the Mount. The important thing is families are talking together without anybody glancing nervously at a wall clock or rushing off to a meeting or trying to catch an ESPN sports roundup.

Using Creativity

Amid a world in technological overdrive, camping brings us back to the basics. At home, our imaginations are rendered nearly useless by computers and gadgets and gizmos. In the woods, we're forced to use our creativity. To improvise. To work together as a team. To figure out how to get Mom's sunglasses off the bottom of the lake, 12 feet down.

When you're camping, you appreciate things easily taken for granted at home, like a bowl of chocolate ice cream and washing your face with warm water. And it doesn't take Nintendo to capture a child's imagination. Instead, children invent their own games, whether it's collecting sticks, damming a stream or playing Mutiny on the Bounty aboard an alligator-shaped air mattress.

We learn things while camping—not only how to whittle a hot-dog stick but, say, what it means to be honest. Once, while fishing with my father, people in nearby boats had caught their legal limits. "We're starting on our second limit," they yelled.

When my father and I limited out, he started the motor (on the 16th pull) and headed for shore. Though such things may seem insignificant at the time, sons remember them.

I remember the day my father let me steer our boat across the lake for the first time; it was a vote of confidence from the man who raised me, a sort of rite-of-passage from boyhood to manhood.

And I remember the night we were asleep in the tent when our dog Jet started barking wildly, bothered by something in our camp. My mother was sure it was a bear. Dad was thinking deer; me, Bigfoot. In fact, it was my father's underwear, hanging on a clothes-line, eerily silhouetted in the light of a full moon.

As we grow from children to adults, we tuck such memories away and forget them, like photographs stowed in an attic. But every now and then, we remember the feel of piercing the cool water with a swan dive, the smell of bacon and eggs on the camp stove, the sound of an ax splitting the evening's firewood. And we want our children to feel and smell and hear those same things.

It isn't important that we have the perfect experiences while camping. Or that we're super campers, those folks whose boat motors start on the first pull and whose air mattresses never go flat during the night. What matters is that we spend time communicating with each other, communicating with God and enjoying this amazing creation of His called Earth.

What's important is simply being together, as my family was two years ago at a campground called Denny Creek. The thunder sounded like boulders colliding in the sky. Rain began pelting our tent. My sons looked to me, seeking reassurance. What I told them marked yet another rite-of-passage for me, not from boy to man, but from son to father.

"Ah, it's just a squall," I said. "It'll pass in no time."

Bob Welch is the features editor at the *Eugene Register-Guard* in Eugene, Oregon.

Enhance the Romance, Intimacy, and Communication in Your Marriage

If you've enjoyed the practical child-rearing advice found in *Raising Them Right* and would love to see something as applicable for yourself, then we've got the book for you! Chock-full of relationship-building tips from favorite *Focus on the Family* magazine articles, ***The Focus on the Family Guide to Growing a Healthy Marriage*** features the wisdom and humor of leading communicators like Dr. James Dobson, Patsy Clairmont, Gary Smalley, John Trent, Ph.D., and many more. This handy guide will prove so helpful, you'll want two—so you won't have to lend your only copy!

Visit your favorite Christian bookstore today.

Parental Guidance

Close-ups and commentaries on the latest music, movies, television and advertisements directed toward young people. Parents, as well as youthleaders, teachers and pastors will benefit from this indispensable newsletter.

All magazines are published monthly except where otherwise noted. For more information regarding these and other resources, please call Focus on the Family at (719) 531-5181, or write to us at Focus on the Family, Colorado Springs, CO 80995.